D1738561

The HF Group
Indiana Plant
EG 055012 3 35 00

6/21/2006

CULTURE SMART!
PHILIPPINES

Graham and Yvonne Colin-Jones

Graphic Arts Center Publishing®

First published in Great Britain 2004
by Kuperard, an imprint of Bravo Ltd.

Copyright © 2004 Kuperard

All rights reserved. No part of this publication may be reprinted or reproduced, stored in a retrieval system, or transmitted in any form or by any means without prior permission in writing from the Publishers.

Series Editor Geoffrey Chesler
Design DW Design

Simultaneously published in the U.S.A. and Canada
by Graphic Arts Center Publishing Company
P. O. Box 10306, Portland, OR 97296-0306

Library of Congress Cataloging-in-Publication Data

Colin-Jones, Graham.
Philippines : a quick guide to customs and etiquette / Graham and Yvonne Colin-Jones.
    p. cm. — (Culture smart!)
Includes bibliographical references and index.
ISBN 1-55868-837-4 (pbk. : alk. paper)
1. Philippines—Social life and customs. 2. Etiquette—Philippines.
3. National characteristics, Philippine. I. Colin-Jones, Yvonne. II. Title.
III. Series.

DS663.C64 2004

959.904'8—dc22

2004003133

Printed in Hong Kong

Cover image: Boats on the Sulu Sea, Zamboanga.
Travel Ink/Abbie Enock

> **CultureShock!Consulting** and **Culture Smart!** guides both contribute to and regularly feature in the weekly travel program "Fast Track" on BBC World TV.

About the Authors

GRAHAM COLIN-JONES is British by birth, a linguist by training, and an international civil servant by profession. He is also the author of books on English grammar, business letter writing, and report writing. He has lived and worked overseas for twenty-two years and has experienced the realities of living and working in Asian cultures, including fifteen years in the Philippines.

YVONNE QUAHE COLIN-JONES is Singaporean by birth, a sociologist by training, and a cross-cultural trainer and relocation professional. She is also an author of the book *We Remember: Cameos of Pioneer Life*, a social history of Singapore using oral history as a medium of documentation.
She has lived most of her life overseas.

Other Books in the Series

- Culture Smart! Australia
- Culture Smart! Britain
- Culture Smart! China
- Culture Smart! Finland
- Culture Smart! France
- Culture Smart! Germany
- Culture Smart! Greece
- Culture Smart! Hong Kong
- Culture Smart! Korea
- Culture Smart! India
- Culture Smart! Italy
- Culture Smart! Ireland
- Culture Smart! Japan
- Culture Smart! Mexico
- Culture Smart! Netherlands
- Culture Smart! Poland
- Culture Smart! Russia
- Culture Smart! Singapore
- Culture Smart! Spain
- Culture Smart! Sweden
- Culture Smart! Switzerland
- Culture Smart! Thailand
- Culture Smart! USA

Other titles are in preparation. For more information,
contact: info@kuperard.co.uk

The publishers would like to thank **CultureShock!Consulting** for its help in researching and developing the concept for this series.

CultureShock!Consulting

We are all likely at some time to be dealing with other cultures—foreign visitors at home, e-mails from abroad, overseas sales agents, multicultural teams within our organization, or a new foreign management structure.

CultureShock!Consulting creates tailor-made seminars and consultancy programs to meet all types of corporate, public sector, and individual intercultural needs. It provides pre- and post-assignment programs, as well as ongoing "in-the-field" counseling worldwide.

For details, see www.cultureshockconsulting.com

contents

Map of the Philippines	7
Introduction	8
Key Facts	10

Chapter 1: LAND AND PEOPLE — 12
- Geography — 12
- Climate — 13
- The Environment — 14
- Natural Disasters — 16
- A Brief History — 18
- The Pre-Spanish Period — 19
- Spanish Colonization — 21
- The American Period — 28
- The Republic of the Philippines — 33
- The Marcos Years — 36
- The Philippines Today — 39

Chapter 2: VALUES AND ATTITUDES — 46
- The Family — 46
- A Relationship-Based Society — 50
- *Bahala Na* — 56
- *Mañana*—Filipino Time — 57
- Attitudes to Foreigners — 58
- Making the Right Impression — 59

Chapter 3: RELIGION AND FESTIVALS — 60
- Religion — 60
- Christian Festivals — 63
- *Fiestas* — 68

- Islamic Festivals 72
- Other Celebrations 73

Chapter 4: **THE FILIPINOS AT HOME** **74**
- Housing 74
- Daily Life and Routines 77
- The Family and Children 79
- Family Celebrations 82
- Entertaining 86
- Household Help 89

Chapter 5: **TIME OUT** **94**
- Shopping 94
- Sports and Games 95
- Gambling 100
- Nightlife 101
- Food and Drink 103

Chapter 6: **TRAVEL, HEALTH, AND SAFETY** **106**
- Road Travel and Transportation 106
- Rail 111
- Ferries and Boats 111
- Air 112
- Places to Visit In and Around Manila 113
- Places to Visit Away From Manila 113
- Health 114
- Medical Care 121
- Safety 125
- Conclusion 129

contents

Chapter 7: BUSINESS BRIEFING — **130**
- Office Etiquette and Protocol — 130
- Management Style — 135
- Speeches and Presentations — 141
- The Motivational Address — 142
- Meetings and Negotiations — 144
- Bureaucracy and Corruption — 147
- Women at Work — 149
- Gift Giving — 150
- Conclusion — 151

Chapter 8: COMMUNICATING — **152**
- Languages — 152
- Means of Communication — 157
- Face to Face — 159
- Nonverbal Language — 161

Conclusion — 164
Further Reading — 165
Index — 166

Map of Philippines

introduction

The Philippines, a scattered archipelago of seven thousand islands, appears to be one of the most Westernized countries in Asia. However, the realities of Filipino life are complex, and not immediately evident to the foreign visitor. Many Filipinos work abroad, far from home and their families, and this is of great significance, not only for the families themselves, but countrywide and internationally. Business is not carried out in quite the same way as in the West. There are social situations and ways of behaving that visitors might well misunderstand.

The Philippines has a unique colonial history, which has been described by its inhabitants as "three centuries in the Convent and fifty years in Hollywood"—it was governed by Spain for over three hundred years and by the United States for fifty. As a result, certain Western beliefs are well entrenched and prevalent. Nearly all Filipinos are Roman Catholics, the government is democratically elected, and freedom of speech and education are highly valued.

Underneath the Western veneer, however, lies an Asian soul. Filipinos share many values and attitudes with other Asian people, although the distinctive blend of East and West is subtle, and can sometimes be difficult to fathom. The foreigner who fails to realize that the façade of the English language (in which most signs in Manila are written), fast food, pop music, and rich lawyers does not run deep will soon commit a *faux pas* that may have long-lasting effects.

Side by side with great wealth, much of the country lives in extreme poverty. *Culture Smart! Philippines* looks at the social, economic, and political problems that have brought this about. Despite their material disadvantages, the Filipino people show an amazing resilience. They are warm, charming, and welcoming. Beyond the chaotic traffic jams and heat of Manila there is so much to enjoy and appreciate in the Philippines that the open-minded visitor will be vastly enriched by the experience.

Culture Smart! Philippines also includes among its pages case studies, true stories, and advice on what to expect and how to behave in many different situations. First-time visitors and long-term foreign workers will find an abundance of practical information and key insights into Filipino society and business life that will enable them to make the very most of their time in this unique and intriguing country.

Key Facts

Official Name	*Republika ng Pilipinas* (Republic of the Philippines)	The Philippines is a member of the Asia Pacific Economic Cooperation (APEC) and the Association of Southeast Asian Nations (ASEAN).
Capital City	Manila (on the island of Luzon)	The metropolitan area is referred to as Metro Manila, or for administrative purposes the National Capital Region (NCR). Pop. of Metro Manila: approx. 11 million
Other Main Cities	Baguio (in Luzon); Cebu (in Visayas); Davao (in Mindanao)	
Area	115,800 sq. miles (300,000 sq. km)	7,107 islands
Climate	Tropical, with an average daily maximum temperature of 90° F (32°C).	Summer, from March to May, is the dry season, with an av. daily max. temp. of 92–95° F (33–35°C).
Terrain	Primarily mountainous with narrow to extensive coastal lowlands.	Coastline varies from rugged cliffs to sandy beaches.
Population	Estimated at around 81 million in 2003	Current growth rate is around 2% p.a.
Adult Literacy	Over 95%	Education is highly valued.

Government	Republic since 1946. The current Constitution was promulgated in 1987. President elected for a single term of six years. Senate of 24 members. House of Representatives: maximum permitted members: 250; current: 229	
Language	Filipino (national language); English (second official language)	Many dialects, incl. Tagalog (the basis for Filipino) and Cebuano
Religion	Approx. 85% Catholic; 5% Muslim; 5% Protestant; 5% others	
Media	Several English newspapers are published as well as Filipino ones.	TV and radio stations in both languages
Economy	GDP growth rate (2003) was 4.4%. GDP per capita (2003) was the equiv. of US $4,200	
Currency	Philippine Peso (PHP or P)	1 Peso = 100 centavos. Exchange rate (Jan. 2004) approx. P55 = US $1
Electricity	220 volts is more common; also 110 volts	Two-pronged plugs generally used; three-pronged plugs for certain uses. Adaptors required.
Video/TV	NTSC system VHS replacing Betamax	
Telephone	Country code for the Philippines is 63	City code for Metro Manila is 2
Time	GMT + 8 hrs	

chapter **one**

LAND & PEOPLE

GEOGRAPHY

The Philippine archipelago lies between the Pacific Ocean and the South China Sea, stretching about 1,150 miles (1,850 km) from north to south, and 684 miles (1,100 km) from east to west. It consists of 7,107 islands and islets, only two thousand of which are inhabited. Most of the islands are very small, and the exact number depends on tide and sea level. Thus, although the land area is 115,800 sq. miles (300,000 sq. km), the Philippines covers a wide area of the western Pacific Ocean, being strategically located between Taiwan in the north and Borneo in the south. The islands are grouped into four regions: Luzon to the north, where the capital, Manila, is located; Palawan to the west; the Visayas in the center; and Mindanao to the south.

Scientists believe that the Philippine Islands were separated from the Asian continent about sixty million years ago. Volcanic activity and tectonic changes continued to occur, and today the country is still liable to be affected by earthquakes and eruptions from its two hundred active volcanoes.

The Philippines is a country of great natural beauty, with majestic mountain ranges in the interior; dense rain forests; fertile plains and valleys; and glorious beaches, lapped by a turquoise sea, along its rugged coastline.

CLIMATE

The climate is typically tropical, with three distinct seasons.

The dry cool season runs from November to February. "Cool," however, is a relative word: to northern Europeans the weather is always hot. Even in the coolest month of January the daytime temperature in Manila rarely falls below 73°F (nearly 23°C), and you can swim in the sea all year-round. In fact, Christmas and New Year are the best times to go to the beach, because it will be less crowded than in the dry hot season, with

weather like a northern European summer. For much cooler weather, you can go to Baguio, in the mountains of Luzon, where the temperature can fall as low as 50°F (10°C) in the evenings.

The dry hot season, known as summer, runs from March to May. The weather suddenly gets hotter in early March, with winds spreading dust everywhere. Air-conditioning becomes a necessity to escape the heat, especially in April and May, when the temperature reaches 95°F (35°C).

The wet hot season runs from June to October. From June to September, the rain can be heavy and persistent over several days, resulting in extensive flooding. By October, it generally consists of thundery showers, often in the early evening. During these months, it is usually a little less hot than in summer, but more humid.

There are regional variations to these seasons. The heavy rains are associated with the prevailing southwest monsoon, and therefore the southeast coast of Luzon may be drier during the wet season and wetter during the summer months.

THE ENVIRONMENT

The Philippine government and many concerned influential people are making strenuous efforts to protect the environment. Regrettably, the value and importance of this is not yet generally appreciated. Filipinos are primarily concerned about their own family unit and financial interests, rather than the welfare of the general public or the environment. Factories in Manila continue to discharge waste into the Pasig River, and the goverment's aims to clean up the waters have only partially been achieved.

Over the past fifty years, extensive logging has resulted in the destruction of more than 90 percent of the original forest growth followed by a number of catastrophic landslides. There is now a law prohibiting all unauthorized logging.

Given its beautiful beaches, warm sea, and coral reefs, tourism could be a major source of income for the country. However, some reefs have been destroyed by illegal fishing techniques. Fishermen are now taught that destroying the reefs will have a serious long-term effect on their livelihood. Despite past damage, the reefs continue to provide wonderful opportunities for scuba diving, and the vast range of fish, from sharks to manta rays and the dugong (sea cow), will ensure that visitors will continue to flock to Philippine waters for years to come.

Overall, the benefits of education are beginning to be seen, with recycling of garbage in certain areas of Manila and greater concern for the environment, including the beautiful seas and flourishing forests. NGOs and other concerned groups have played a leading role in this campaign, and it is hoped that progress in this direction will continue.

NATURAL DISASTERS
Volcanoes and Earthquakes

As recently as 1991, Mount Pinatubo, on the island of Luzon, erupted, killing nearly 900 people. The deaths were largely caused by *lahar* (volcanic mud), which flowed down the mountainside and destroyed everything in its path. Since Mount Pinatubo is 100 miles (160 km) from Manila, residents were not alarmed when eruptions started on Monday, June 10, but on Saturday came the devastating eruption. It was dark in Manila by 4:30 p.m., and ash began to fall. The interesting phenomenon became a matter of personal concern when people were advised to

wear masks. Then it was announced that Manila airport would remain closed for three days while the runway was cleared; the danger was that ash would be sucked into the engines. More than ten years later, the devastation can still be seen, with dried *lahar* up to the rooftops of destroyed houses, and every year during the rainy season bridges are seriously damaged as more *lahar* is carried down the mountainside. Other volcanoes also threaten to erupt at frequent intervals, especially Mount Mayon, in the south of Luzon.

Another recent natural disaster was the 1990 earthquake, which killed over 1,600 people in northern Luzon. Even in Manila buildings shook and developed cracks. Fault lines run through the city, and after the 1995 Kobe earthquake, in Japan, pillars supporting flyovers in Manila were further strengthened to withstand tremors.

Typhoons

Every year between May and December at least thirty typhoons pass across the Philippines. They do not normally affect the southern island of Mindanao, but often bring devastation to the rest of the country. Typhoons until August tend to go north toward Hong Kong, often passing across the remote Batanes islands located north of Luzon. From September, the likelihood of a typhoon making a direct hit on Manila increases. Current advances in predicting the course of typhoons means that storm signals are announced in plenty of time. Thus, schools and offices are closed when a serious typhoon is approaching, to give people time to return home safely.

Typhoons may cause damage to power lines, leading to power outages (cuts), known in the Philippines as "brownouts." A recent brownout affecting the whole of Luzon was brought about by jellyfish, which had caused a blockage. Despite the frustrations, the Filipinos were able to laugh, and still talk about this incident.

The Filipinos accept typhoons and other natural disasters with the words "*Bahala Na*," which mean, "Leave it to God," or, "If this is what God has dealt us, so be it." (See page 56.) They have a remarkable capacity to pick themselves up and start again, even in the face of ruined homes and crops and seriously damaged infrastructure. Their resilience is amazing.

A BRIEF HISTORY

In order to understand Filipino culture, it helps to have some knowledge of the country's history. Successive waves of invaders and immigrants have influenced the molding of the Filipino mindset.

What is critical to an understanding of modern Filipinos is the recognition that despite their ethnic and religious differences they all share an essentially Asian value system, based on the importance of relationships. Later Spanish and American influences may have left their mark, but Filipino roots are Asian.

THE PRE-SPANISH PERIOD
Origins

It is believed that the aboriginal inhabitants of the Philippine Islands, who arrived over 25,000 years ago, were pygmies related to the Andaman Islanders, the Samang of Malaysia, and various New Guinea tribes. They are considered ancestors of the Aeta, or Negrito, tribes, both terms referring to small, dark-skinned people. They crossed from the Asian mainland over the remaining land bridges and settled in the lowland forests. Being fierce warriors, they fought with later settlers, but, unable to overcome the firearms of the Spanish, they moved away, mainly into the mountain regions. The Luzon Aeta in particular were affected by the Pinatubo eruption, with their ancestral lands being buried in ash and *lahar*.

Further Aeta migration occurred about 5,000 years ago, and so there are tribes in various parts of the Philippines with slightly different names, and different religious beliefs. Some believe in a Supreme Being who rules over lesser spirits, while others are animists. Those Pinatubo Aeta who believe in Apo Namalyan, the most powerful spirit, say that his anger at the digging of the Philippine National Oil company led to the eruption of Mount Pinatubo.

From about 3000 BCE onward many other peoples crossed the seas and settled in the islands.

Since these included Indonesians and Malays, it explains why Filipinos are considered to be of the same stock.

The earliest inhabitants were hunter-gatherers. With Neolithic technology and the development of basic tools, forests were cleared and agriculture begun. In the Metal Age (c. 700-200 BCE) tools became more advanced, and knives were used to cut bamboo, from which huts and utensils were made. Knives of this type (*bolo*) are still common in rural areas, and are dangerous weapons.

The Age of Trade

Subsequently, from the ninth century onward, traders from China, India, Arabia, and Japan began to visit the islands. Chinese porcelain, silk, colored beads, gold, and ivory were traded for forest and marine products such as teak, rattan, pearls, and precious shells. Archaeological excavation has unearthed a huge array of Chinese plates and bowls, dated to a period between the Song and Ming dynasties, between the tenth and seventeenth centuries. The Chinese have continued to trade and also migrate to the Philippines down the centuries, and many of today's leading businessmen are of Chinese descent.

The influence of the Arabian traders commenced in the tenth century, when they sought alternative trading routes, having been expelled from southern Chinese ports. The Islamic religion began to spread in the thirteenth century, and this is particularly evident in the southern island of Mindanao.

SPANISH COLONIZATION

On March 16, 1521, Ferdinand Magellan landed in what is now the Eastern Visayas, on the uninhabited island of Homonhon, and then sailed on to Limasawa, where, on Easter Sunday, March 31, he celebrated Mass on the shore. Having proceeded to Cebu, he was welcomed by the ruler, Rajah Humabon, who allowed the Spanish to trade with his people. On April 14, Humabon and his family converted to Christianity and were baptized. The other chieftains of Cebu, who recognized Humabon as their king, also converted to Christianity, except for Lapu-Lapu, the ruler of Mactan Island (now the location of Cebu's airport and connected to Cebu by two bridges).

Magellan and Humabon joined forces to destroy Lapu-Lapu. On April 27, 1521, Magellan took his men to Mactan to attack those of Lapu-Lapu. However, he was killed in action. He had miscalculated the tides and had not appreciated the consequences of wearing armor in hand-to-hand fighting in the water. Humabon then turned on the Spanish forces and contributed to their defeat.

The problem of kinship rivalry and regionalism is a recurring theme in the history of the Philippines, and the Spanish would later exploit local divisions to good effect. The failure to unite continues to hamper economic and political progress at both local and national levels.

The Spanish were still determined to gain access to the riches of the East. Further expeditions were undertaken during the following twenty-five years, and the islands were named Las Islas Felipinas after Prince Felipe, who later became Philip II of Spain.

The Spanish king gave instructions to his viceroy in Mexico, Miguel Lopez de Legaspi, to colonize the islands. Legaspi and his fleet reached Cebu in 1565, took it by force, and built strong fortifications. When food ran short he went further north, to the natural harbor of Maynilad, but met with resistance from the ruler. In the following year, 1571, Legaspi returned with a stronger force and took control of Maynilad.

By 1580, the Spanish controlled most of the islands, which remained a crown colony of Spain for over three hundred years. The colony was under the administration of the viceroy of Mexico until 1821, when Mexico achieved independence.

From then until 1898 it was under the direct control of the government in Madrid. What is the legacy of those three centuries of Spanish rule?

Conversion to Christianity

One of the main aims of colonization was to convert the natives to Christianity. Its success can be seen in the fact that over 90 percent of Filipinos are Christian, and the vast majority of those are Catholic. On Saturdays and Sundays, the churches are full, as the Filipinos take their faith very seriously.

Introduction of Central Government

The primary social unit had previously been the *barangay,* the village community, which was composed of a kinship group of up to a hundred families with a respected chief. Disputes between *barangays* used to arise, and were often settled by bloodshed. Although the *barangay* remained an important feature of Filipino society at the local level, with the *barangay* captain being a man of influence, the Spanish introduced the concept of central government. The head of the government was the Governor-General, appointed by the King of

Spain. He was also commander-in-chief of the army and President of the Supreme Court (Royal Audencia), and he had authority over the Church.

The Philippines was governed by special laws, which consisted of royal decrees, and Spanish laws that the King extended to cover the Philippines. However, the Spanish administrators believed in their superiority and expected to be recompensed accordingly, particularly for favors. Corruption became a way of life.

The Landowners

Having conquered the country, Legaspi gave large pieces of land to Spanish nationals, religious orders, and soldiers, in return for their efforts in the conquest or in Christianization. These pieces of land, together with the inhabitants, were called *encomiendas*. The intention was that landowners would be responsible for the spiritual and physical welfare of the inhabitants living on their land, the latter making payments in cash or kind. The landowners became rich and their abuses resulted in so much dissatisfaction that the system was abolished in 1674.

In due course, the Spanish intermarried with the native Filipinos, giving rise to the *mestizo* class. The *mestizos*, who generally look more European, were eventually given the right to buy and own land. In the mid-1800s, there was an agricultural boom, and the landowning *mestizos* became particularly wealthy. Chinese *mestizos* also became landowners. Today, certain *mestizo* families own huge tracts of prime land in Manila and run thriving businesses.

Taxation and Forced Labor

Until 1884, every Filipino family or unmarried adult was required to pay a head tax to Spain, and the tax collectors became wealthy. People were also obliged to pay a church tax and forced to work for nothing on repairing roads and bridges, building ships, and cutting down trees. This, and even having their rations taken by the officials, caused great anger, which led to the uprising against the Spaniards.

Education and Urbanization

With the aim of converting the people to Christianity, the Spanish brought various missionary orders, including the Augustines, the Jesuits, and the Dominicans, to their new colony. These orders founded schools, hospitals, and churches, and people were strongly encouraged to move into the towns, where these facilities were available. Even today, the best educational establishments are supported by religious orders.

Education under the Spanish introduced the Filipinos to the Roman alphabet and the Spanish

language, bringing them closer to
Europe in terms of language,
culture, and thinking. The high
level of literacy among Filipinos
placed the country intellectually
ahead of the rest of the region.

The construction of the churches led to the
development of a Western style of architecture,
together with Catholic sculpture and paintings.

The Rise of Nationalism

At various times during the Spanish occupation,
the Filipino people had rebelled against their
harsh rulers, but they had been ruthlessly
crushed. However, as the nineteenth century
progressed, so the Philippines was opened up to
Western culture and ideas, and the beginnings of
a middle class could be seen. The national hero
and polymath Jose Rizal, who had been educated
in Europe, in 1886 wrote a novel, *Noli Me Tangere*
("Touch Me Not"), describing conditions under
Spanish rule and the abuses of the friars. The
Spanish remained opposed to any significant
reforms, however, and certain Filipinos, inspired
by Rizal's writings, determined to break free from
the cruel Spanish rule, some being prepared to go
beyond his nonviolent approach. In 1892, a secret
society, the *Katipunan* ("society"), was founded by
Andres Bonifacio, a warehouse clerk from a poor

background who had educated himself by reading Rizal and French revolutionary writers.

In August 1896, an informant told the Spanish authorities about the *Katipunan*, and some *Katipunan* members were arrested and executed. This sparked a violent revolution, led by Emilio Aguinaldo, from a well-connected family in Cavite, south of Manila. Initially, he had some successes, and the execution of Rizal on December 30, 1896, provided further impetus to the revolutionaries. Jose Rizal is regarded as a martyr, having shed his blood for the nation.

A dispute then arose between Aguinaldo and Bonifacio as to who should lead the revolutionary government, which ended with the revolutionary court condemning Bonifacio to death. The revolutionaries then suffered defeats and agreed to a peace, with Aguinaldo going into exile in Hong Kong.

Even today outside observers ask why Filipinos seem so often to "shoot themselves in the foot." At the moment when they could be successful and move forward, they are brought to their knees by a personal or family dispute. This is because kinship ties are stronger than national interests; a personal affront goes deep and is not easily forgiven, and the kinship group rallies around the aggrieved party, resulting in retaliation and a worsening of the relationship.

THE AMERICAN PERIOD

In Hong Kong, Emilio Aguinaldo met with U.S. naval and foreign office officials and won their support for the struggle against Spain. The United States was already backing Cuban revolt against Spanish rule, and it made sense to support the Filipinos too.

In May 1898 Aguinaldo returned to the Philippines and on June 12 (which is now a national holiday) declared independence. When his American allies arrived in August, Aguinaldo was approaching Manila. However, the Spanish Governor secretly negotiated with the U.S. commander for a mock battle to be fought without the involvement of Filipino troops. This enabled him to surrender with dignity and avoid being massacred by the Filipino forces.

In September Aguinaldo convened a congress at Malolos, a town nearly 19 miles (about 30 km) north of Manila, and the Malolos Constitution was promulgated on January 21, 1899, establishing the First Republic of the Philippines.

Meanwhile, discussions were held in Paris between the Americans and Spanish, and on December 10, 1898, the Treaty of Paris was signed, making the former the new rulers of the Philippines, and also of Guam and Puerto Rico. In return the Americans made a gift of $20 million to the Spanish; the Filipinos regarded this as an outrage, noting that although the Americans claimed to be opposed to slavery, they bought whole countries together with their inhabitants.

Aguinaldo soon realized that he had been duped, and that the United States did not intend to grant self-government to the Philippines. Thus, the Philippine-American war started in February 1899, resulting in much bloodshed among both fighters and civilians. Once Aguinaldo was captured in March 1901, the cause was lost, but a guerrilla campaign continued until 1903. By that time, there was a desire for peace, except in Mindanao, where the Muslims continued to resist American rule. With peace established, the Americans introduced a different style of rule from the Spanish, bringing about reforms in the areas of government, education, and health. Importantly, they introduced the concept of democracy and freedom of speech.

In the early 1930s, as a result of the Great Depression, many U.S. politicians sought to protect U.S. interests, including agriculture. One measure was to sever colonial relationships, and in 1934 Manuel Quezon went to Washington, D.C. to negotiate the Tydings-McDuffie Act. Under this Act, a new Constitution was drawn up, and a Commonwealth government was established with Manuel Quezon as President, with the intention that the Philippines would be self-governing after ten years. With democracy came freedom of speech, and the Filipinos learned to express themselves strongly in support of their rights. Recent political rallies and the media provide ample evidence that freedom of speech is a prominent feature of Philippine society today.

Even more than the Spanish, the Americans ensured that the Filipinos received a good and broad education. Coeducational schools were introduced, and the focus was no longer on religious teaching, but on literature, arts, and sciences, as well as the English language. Today English is widely spoken throughout the Philippines, while Spanish remains the language of the *mestizos*. Knowledge of English has enabled Filipinos to find jobs in many English-speaking countries overseas.

The Philippines also benefited from medical advances in the United States. Common diseases such as smallpox and cholera had been a serious problem, but the Americans improved sanitation and introduced a health system for the people.

The improvements in all these areas under the Americans made a very positive impression on the Filipino people. Many Filipinos have U.S. passports or green cards, and most of the population dream of living in the United States one day. On the other hand, some Filipinos also resent the influence and controlling nature of the Americans, and this led to the decision to remove the U.S. bases in the 1990s. The popularity of American fast food and movies is offset by the frequency of demonstrations outside the U.S. embassy. The love-hate relationship between the Filipinos and Americans is set to continue.

The Second World War

As President of the Commonwealth government, Manuel Quezon set about organizing the defense of the Philippines, with General Douglas MacArthur as his special advisor. However, with the military rise of Japan, MacArthur was recalled to active duty as commander of the U.S. Armed Forces in the Asia-Pacific region.

The attack on Pearl Harbor in December 1941 was immediately followed by the Japanese invasion of the Philippines. Despite the leadership of MacArthur, the Japanese prevailed, and in April 1942 they occupied Bataan, a peninsula between Manila Bay and the South China Sea. This resulted in the "Death March" of 75,000 prisoners (American and Filipino, who had fought side by side) in searing heat to a prison camp 55 miles (90 km) away. Of these, 10,000 died or were killed by their captors en route, and a further 20,000 died in the camp due to malnutrition and disease. This march is remembered each year, and the atrocities committed by the occupying Japanese have not been forgotten by the older generation.

The Americans and Filipinos made a last desperate stand on Corregidor, an island in Manila Bay, and shortly before the final surrender General MacArthur followed orders and was airlifted out of the country for strategic reasons, as was Manuel Quezon, who set up a Philippine government in exile. The defending troops ran out of supplies, and were forced to surrender to the Japanese. A visit to Corregidor is essential to appreciate this period of Filipino history.

During the Japanese occupation, a Philippine government (the Second Republic) was established under Jose Laurel, but it was merely a puppet regime under the supervision of the Japanese, who maltreated the Filipino people. Most of the Philippine elite served under the Japanese, for various reasons. Some believed they were protecting their people from further harsh treatment; some were protecting their families (very important for Filipinos); some were serving their personal interests; some believed that Philippine nationalism would be advanced by solidarity with fellow Asians; and some collaborated with the Japanese only to pass on information to the Allies.

On the other hand, there was a resistance movement, composed of Americans and Filipinos, which conducted guerrilla attacks against the Japanese. In addition, in rural areas organized resistance came from the poor peasants, who were known as the Huk (short for Hukbalahap, in turn the abbreviated form for *Hukbong Bayan Laban Sa Hapon*, meaning People's Anti-Japanese Army). It is estimated that over a million Filipinos died as a result of the war.

When General MacArthur left the country on instruction from Washington, he uttered the famous words, "I shall return." Sure enough, in October 1944 he landed in Leyte, at the head of the Allied forces, and by February 1945 liberation had been achieved.

THE REPUBLIC OF THE PHILIPPINES

The Filipinos were pleased to be liberated, but recognized the inability of the Americans to defend them in the first place. This was a spur to their demand for independence, which America granted while retaining a long-term lease on their military and naval bases.

The choice of first president of an independent Philippines was between Sergio Osmeña, the aging President of the Commonwealth government who had returned from exile with

MacArthur, and Manuel Roxas, who had served in the pro-Japanese government early in the war, but later joined the Allies.
Feeling his age, Osmeña did not campaign strongly, and on July 4, 1946, the Third Republic of the Philippines was established under the presidency of Roxas.

The destruction and devastation caused by the war was extensive, and the task of rebuilding was huge. However, widespread bribery and corruption affected the rebuilding process. Also, patriots who had resisted the Japanese received no preferential treatment over collaborators, and this caused great resentment.

The rich landowners had generally collaborated with the Japanese, while their poor tenant farmers had joined the Huk resistance movement. Thus, after the war, the tenants no longer felt any deference toward their landlords and resisted exploitation. The Huk leader, Luis Taruc, was arrested by MacArthur as a Communist, and the Huks were ordered to hand over their weapons. President Roxas was unpopular, first, because early in the war he had been a collaborator, and second, he had initially refused to introduce laws to increase the percentage of the harvest that should be given to tenants. In anger and frustration, many tenant farmers joined the Huk movement, which changed its name to the People's Liberation Army.

Despite conciliatory efforts by the incoming President Elpidio Quirino, including the offer of an amnesty, the Huks grew in number and strength as the government became increasingly unpopular. Seizing the opportunity, the Communists of the Partido Kommunista ng Pilipinas (PKP) joined the Huk rebellion, and by 1950 posed a serious threat to the government. Open hostilities continued until 1954, by which time the Americans had provided additional assistance to crush the Communists. In addition, individual Huks had perpetrated atrocities, such as the assassination of the widow of President Quezon, and so the movement lost sympathy with the people. Tired from years of fighting, the tenant farmers returned home, hopeful that life would improve under the new President Ramon Magsaysay, who gave land and tools to those who left the Huk movement.

Unfortunately, Magsaysay was killed in an airplane crash in 1957. His successor, Carlos P. Garcia, introduced an austerity program discouraging extravagant lifestyles, fought corruption (with only modest success), and introduced the Filipino First Policy, which gave priority to Filipinos over foreigners in the acquisition of land and capital and in the operation of business, trade, and industry.

In the election of 1961, Garcia's vice president, Diosdado Macapagal, stood against him and triumphed. A man of honesty and integrity, he fought graft and corruption, introduced a land reform law, which freed many poor peasants from the burden of tenancy, and encouraged free enterprise to stimulate the economy.

THE MARCOS YEARS

In 1965, Ferdinand Marcos defeated Macapagal and became President at a time when the Philippines was regarded as the most Westernized country in the region, and well before the tiger economies of Singapore, Taiwan, and Hong Kong had taken off. At first, the Marcos administration was highly regarded: he spent all available

resources on development and unified the country through the construction of bridges, ports, and roads, but gradually dissatisfaction increased. The Communist Party of the Philippines (CPP) was founded in 1968 by Jose Maria Sison, and the following year the CPP guerrilla movement, known as the New People's Army (NPA) was formed with a number of former Huk fighters. The PKP and CPP clashed over ideology, the former being Soviet backed and the latter being Maoist, and in due course the PKP faded from prominence.

In Mindanao, the Moros (Filipino Muslims) had always resisted the Spanish and Americans. After the Philippines attained independence in 1946 they sought separate independence, but took no decisive action in that regard. In the late 1960s, when more Christians began to move to Mindanao, political tension increased, and armed gangs created turmoil. In the 1970s the Moro National Liberation Front (MNLF) was formed to fight for an independent Moro nation. During the 1970s, an estimated 50,000 people, military and civilian, were killed in the struggle.

The 1935 Constitution did not permit a third presidential term in office, and as his popularity declined Marcos realized that the only way to remain in power was to declare martial law. In 1972, he claimed that law and order had deteriorated and that the Communists posed a serious threat, and on this basis he declared martial law. Freedom of speech was curtailed and opponents were imprisoned or exiled, one of those being Senator Benigno Aquino. During this period, the Marcos cronies made their millions, corruption became a way of life, and Imelda Marcos, the First Lady, became infamous for her extravagance. She tried to encourage the arts, and was responsible for the construction of the

Cultural Center of the Philippines on reclaimed land in Manila Bay.

Under pressure, Marcos lifted martial law in 1981, but the opposition to his presidency only increased. In 1983, despite warnings about his safety, Benigno Aquino flew back from the U.S.A., and was assassinated as he left the plane. Elections were scheduled for February 7, 1986, and Corazon Aquino, his widow, was persuaded to represent the opposition groups and to run against Marcos.

People Power

On February 8, 1986, Corazon (Cory) Aquino declared herself the winner on the basis of an independent tally, but on February 15 the Philippine National Assembly declared Marcos the victor. It was evident that there had been large-scale manipulation of the count. The people could not accept a Marcos triumph, and a week later hundreds of thousands marched in the streets in a show of "people power." They walked up the main thoroughfare, Epifanio de los Santos Avenue, known as EDSA, to the military camp, and demanded that Marcos stand down. They came in peace, carrying rosaries, and praying. The military in their tanks could have mown them down; but key individuals Fidel Ramos (Chief of Staff) and Juan Ponce Enrile (Defense Minister), chose to turn against Marcos and support the people, and the army followed their lead. A dictator was overthrown without a drop of blood being shed. The Filipino people are proud of what they achieved that day. They continue to believe in "people power," backed up by prayer.

THE PHILIPPINES TODAY

On February 25, 1986, Ferdinand Marcos went into exile in the U.S.A., and Cory Aquino became President. But her early years in office were riddled with coup attempts, orchestrated either by Marcos loyalists or by those who saw an opportunity to take power for themselves. Aquino failed to kick start the economy, and made little investment in the country's infrastructure. Hampered by differences within her cabinet and by natural disasters (earthquake and volcanic eruption), she made one positive achievement—the restoration of democracy.

In an attempt to prevent the possibility of a return to a dictatorial regime, the 1987 Constitution of the Philippines states that "The Philippines is a democratic and republican state. Sovereignty resides in the people and all government authority emanates from them." It also permits only a single term of six years in office as President of the Republic.

The Constitution enshrines a system of government similar to that of the U.S.A. The legislature, the Congress of the Philippines, consists of a Senate and House of Representatives. There are 24 Senators and a maximum of 250 members of the House of Representatives.

The next president was Fidel Ramos (1992–8), hero of the EDSA revolution. He had to deal with the problem of serious power shortages, which resulted in areas of Manila being without power for up to eight hours per day during the hot summer months. The effect on industry, let alone the low morale of the people, was devastating. However, he took swift action, and the economy made considerable progress.

The 1998 presidential election was won by Joseph Estrada (Erap), a former actor famous for his heroic screen performances as a champion of the poor. Unfortunately, real-life responsibilities proved too demanding, and he relied on his cronies to advise him. Corruption grew, and people became dissatisfied. Eventually, Erap himself was charged with corruption, and evidence against him was mounting. However, he had sufficient support in the Senate to win a major decision regarding the non-opening of an envelope believed to contain information that would further incriminate him. As a result, the people took to EDSA again, encouraged by the

Church, led by Cardinal Sin, and former presidents Cory Aquino and Fidel Ramos.

EDSA II

The key moment in this second display of "people power," also called EDSA II, or *EDSA Dos*, occurred when the Defense Secretary, together with the military and police, voiced their support for the Vice President, Gloria Macapagal-Arroyo. Then the Supreme Court ruled that, in view of the circumstances surrounding President Estrada, it would not be unconstitutional for the Vice President to take over the Presidency for the remainder of Erap's term of office.

Thus, on January 20, 2001, Gloria Macapagal-Arroyo (GMA) was sworn in as President, as her father had been in 1961, and has fought hard to bring integrity back into government. The economy has continued to struggle, but there has been a global economic downturn.

The problem of Mindanao has faced all Manila governments. Armed conflict and acts of terrorism have limited the amount of foreign investment there and exacerbated the poverty of the people. The Moro Islamic Liberation Front (MILF), a breakaway group from the MNLF, has continued the violent struggle for separation, despite the creation in 1990 of the Autonomous Region for Muslim Mindanao (ARMM).

In 1991, the Abu Sayyaf Group (meaning "Bearer of the Sword" in Arabic) broke away from the MNLF. This group has close links with international fundamentalist organizations such as Al-Qaeda. Based in the islands south of Mindanao (Basilan, Sulu, and Tawi-Tawi), the ASG claims to want an Iranian-style Islamic state in Mindanao, and uses terror tactics primarily for financial gain.

From time to time, bombs go off in airports or shopping centers, with responsibility ascribed to any one of several separatist groups opposed to the government. President GMA is making a determined effort to bring about a lasting peace.

The Filipinos are generally easygoing, and have coped for centuries with poverty and corruption. They want peace and a more equitable society. Will they achieve what they so richly deserve? Regrettably, the divisions within the elite are great and, whoever wins an election, the opposition will do its utmost to ensure the failure of the government. Furthermore, the fostering of a greater public conscience is necessary if people are willingly to pay their taxes, and graft and corruption are finally to be eliminated. Until there is greater unity and a deep desire for a more equitable society, the Philippines will have a struggle to break free of its shackles of poverty.

Transfer of Power, Filipino-Style

There were six unsuccessful attempted coups against Cory Aquino, and two successful displays of "people power" on EDSA to overthrow corrupt and, in one case, despotic presidents. Yet there were very few casualties, because no real animosity existed between those involved. There was no desire to shed blood, and most shooting was deliberately over the heads of the enemy.

One of the saddest stories of the 1989 coup attempt led by Gringo Honasan (a popular military hero) was the death of a soldier in his tank when a grenade was thrown at it. The soldier who threw the grenade was the brother of the one killed. It is also worth noting that Gringo Honasan, after a short time in prison, is now a Senator; the people had focused on his previous achievements, and did not condemn him for the attempted coup.

The rally at EDSA in January 2001 against the Senate over Joseph Estrada epitomizes the Filipinos' approach to life. It demonstrated their belief in the freedom of speech (politicians, priests, and community leaders made speeches against the decision of the Senate). It showed their love of entertainment (musicians performed on stage, the speeches with plenty of jokes were applauded the loudest). It displayed their love of luxury and ostentation (the wealthy took rooms in a four-star hotel behind the EDSA shrine to watch the events on TV and hurry to the stage area when a VIP arrived to make a speech). It showed their optimism (they believed that there would be a peaceful and successful conclusion to their vigil; the Catholic faithful ascribe success to prayer). It demonstrated their aversion to violence (it was a totally peaceful handover of power).

The Economy

The Philippine economy, based primarily on a mixture of agriculture, light industry, and supporting services, deteriorated owing to the 1997 Asian financial crisis. Recovery has been slow, and global economic difficulties, compounded by the war on terrorism, have also affected it; yet the projected GDP growth for 2004 is around 5 percent. Unemployment remains at over 10 percent, however, and the budget deficit has escalated to the equivalent of U.S. $4 billion.

Much of the budget shortfall relates to the poor record on tax collection. The wealthy are reluctant to pay taxes, claiming that because of corruption the money is not utilized effectively. Thus, they evade tax and salve their consciences by giving to social projects for the poor. However, these are often connected to their own extended family, and the help given to those in real need is limited.

An estimated 40 percent of Filipinos live on less than U.S. $2 a day. With 36 percent aged under fifteen, and a population growth rate of 2 percent per annum, the situation does not look encouraging unless further jobs are created. The Protestant President Ramos wanted to control the birth rate, but the Catholic Church opposed it.

The shortage of jobs and the low salaries have resulted in the phenomenon of seven million overseas Filipino workers (OFWs), or overseas contract workers (OCWs). These people range from engineers to nurses to domestic helpers, and remit over U.S. $6 billion per annum—the largest single source of foreign exchange for the country. They live far from their families, whom they support, and may return only once every two or three years. However, this brain drain is a serious loss to the Philippines in terms of vital skills.

The current government promises economic reforms relating to privatization, the tax system, and trade. It also recognizes that peace and stability are prerequisites for sustainable economic growth, and is striving for a peaceful solution in Mindanao and for more constructive dialogue with the NPA.

chapter **two**

VALUES & ATTITUDES

When living and working abroad, it is important to understand the behavior of others whose culture and customs are different from one's own. The following guidelines are an introduction to the views and values of the Filipinos.

THE FAMILY

A Filipino's sense of self is derived from his or her family: "I am who I am because of my family; their success is my success, and my shame is their shame." This mindset has its roots in the former agricultural economy, where many hands were needed on the farm—a situation that still pertains in the rural areas today. The family (*pamilya*) is the most important social unit in the Philippines, a core value, and the ultimate safety net. A Filipino would find it almost impossible to refuse family requests or ignore family obligations.

Traditionally, parents are respected and their

wishes honored. Children usually live at home until they marry. It is not unusual for a wealthy family to live in its own compound, consisting of the main house, where the parents and unmarried children live, and smaller houses built for the married ones. Elderly parents are never left to live alone, and would consider this as one of the most humiliating things that could happen. In fact to a Filipino, the ultimate curse is "to be alone."

Family obligations can be onerous, particularly for those in the lower socioeconomic group. Many people might be totally dependent on one person's wage. The "successful" one is obligated to take care of the others. The eldest child may sacrifice a good education in order to start earning money for the family, and it is not uncommon for a domestic helper or a waiter in a good hotel to be supporting eight or nine people. Typically, a young woman from the provinces will go to work in Manila as a household helper in order to support the whole family and enable her younger siblings to be educated.

Wages in the Philippines are very low, however, and those who wish to do better must attend the right schools and have good connections. Upward social mobility is virtually impossible for those low on the socioeconomic ladder. Hence, a great many Filipinos, both male and female, leave home and family to seek employment overseas. Some leave with very little knowledge of the place they are going to, or even the job they are going to do; mothers leave their young children to become domestic helpers abroad, and return home every three years. When asked why they do this, they always, without exception, answer, "For my family, so that they can have a better future." "Family" does not just mean spouse and children; it includes the extended family of siblings, uncles, aunts, nephews, and nieces.

Airports in the Philippines are always crowded with well-wishers to such an extent that at Manila International Airport only passengers are allowed to enter the terminal. Employees prefer to incur the ire of their boss rather than miss going to the airport to say good-bye to a relative who is leaving the country to work abroad. It is a recognition of the sacrifice, a cementing of the relationship, a giving of face, and a tacit way of saying, "when I am in need I may call on you."

Families are not without conflict, as the reality of human relationships is never smooth. Today the older generation complains about the younger generation's lack of respect and refusal to adhere to traditional values; but kinship unifies, and differences are forgotten in times of extreme need of assistance or if threatened by an "outsider."

Marriage in the Philippines is an alliance of families, particularly in the case of the wealthy and influential, and may serve political affiliations and business interests. It would be difficult to be married into a family where one is not welcome, or whose company one does not enjoy, because there is a lot of "togetherness." Rich families go on holiday together, often abroad, with parents paying for everyone; holiday homes are shared; and Sunday is a day for family get-togethers.

Pamilya can also be perceived, meaning that certain people outside the family are thought of in a familial light. These may be godparents, for example, or people to whom one is closely connected for one reason or another. When a Filipino tells you that someone is his *compadre*, sometimes abbreviated to *pare*, he is saying that a close relationship exists between them. It can be advantageous in a work situation, but it would be extremely difficult for a supervisor to take any disciplinary action against his *compadre*.

Utang na loob, or debt of gratitude, runs deep in Philippine society, and implies loyalty and recognition of a favor. This could involve covering up for a colleague at work, and saving him from losing his job; putting a good word in for a subordinate that results in a promotion; helping someone to get a job in a good company; or providing money for medicine when your helper's child is seriously ill. How do you measure this debt? The general rule of thumb is, "What did I save you from?" A debt of gratitude between families can be carried on for generations. At its heart is reciprocity. This leads to stronger bonding in relationships, and people are expected to take care of each other. On the other hand, it leads to a relationship of patronage. Such ties can take precedence over right and reason.

> ### *"ONE BIG, HAPPY FAMILY"*
> Filipinos function well within a familial setting. Companies know this, and often use the idea to motivate their workers. You will see banners and advertisements using the concept of family, and it is not unusual to find a screen in a company's reception area listing the names of staff members who have a birthday on that day. Check to see if the name of the person you are meeting is there! The management style that most Filipinos best respond to is that of "a firm but caring parent."

A RELATIONSHIP-BASED SOCIETY
In Filipino culture emphasis is placed on smooth interpersonal relationships, with harmony being prized and loss of face avoided. The key concepts here are *pakikisama*, *pakikipagkapwa*, and *hiya*.

Pakikisama can be defined as the desire to be accepted by the group, or the ability to get along. On the positive side, it is a sense of belonging, and is the source of a feeling of "togetherness" in good times and bad, providing material and emotional support. *Pakikisama* also motivates staff to work harder for the common good of the group and provide a very strong support system apart from the family. The downside is that this loyalty prevails in decisions on the right or sensible course to take. The group will not blow the whistle if one of its members breaks the rules. One or more may aid others in wrongdoing. At best, the rest will remain silent.

Closely intertwined with *pakikisama* is *pakikipagkapwa*, which is the strong need for smooth interpersonal relationships. This leads to a cautious handling of conflicts, as a result of which Filipinos seem to be easily forgiving, and are generally very helpful. On the other hand, an issue that really should be sorted out may be deliberately fudged or swept under the carpet, and a "band-aid" solution found. Where a resolution is essential, a traditional go-between may be used—ideally someone who is held in esteem by both parties. Personal interaction always overrides procedures. In an office setting, this often gives undue power to the go-between, and accurate information (which is necessary to good problem solving) is sometimes difficult to obtain or skewed, consciously or otherwise.

Remember that the primary goal of communication is harmony, not the giving and receiving of information, and the answer to most questions is "Yes." "Maybe" and "I will try" are both indicative of "No." A Filipino rarely says "No." However, information and feelings must still be communicated, and this is often done by way of hints, humor, and jokes.

Much has been written about the Asian concept of "loss of face." At its heart lies the simple message, "Please do not make my failures or shortcomings public; I am aware of them."

The values of *hiya* and *amor propio* help to explain this. *Hiya* is a sense of shame. The anthropologist Frank Lynch describes it as "the uncomfortable feeling that accompanies awareness of being in a socially unacceptable position, or performing a socially unacceptable action." It is this *hiya* that makes the Filipino think twice about wrongdoing; but it also constrains him or her in many ways. For instance, there is a hesitancy about asking a supervisor to clarify instructions, whatever the consequences. The Filipino will giggle or grin in an embarrassed way, with downcast eyes, when communicating with someone in a higher position, especially when he or she is unsure or afraid of the other's reaction. This happens frequently between boss and subordinate, and many a frustrated foreigner has found that Filipinos will never ask for extra information, query an unclear instruction, or simply admit that they have made a mistake.

The Technician and the TV

After a storm and a brownout (power outage, or cut), Ian's television, which he had left on standby, was no longer working. It was an imported set, and not one of the more common brands available in the Philippines. However, he found a technician who said he could repair it, and pointed out that it was a 110-volt set. The man took it away. He returned with it a week later, triumphantly telling Ian how good the picture was. He plugged it in and turned it on. Bang!

In the Philippines, many houses have both 110 and 220 power outlets, positioned side by side. They are usually marked, but not very clearly, and the technician had not asked which was which. He guessed, and got it wrong. Ian was amazed that he hadn't simply asked him which outlet to use—but a Filipino would rarely ask such a question. Ian learned the hard way that in future he must take the initiative and provide the necessary information without being asked.

Hiya also restrains a colleague from openly disagreeing with another, especially in public. It also results in great sensitivity to criticism, even constructive criticism. The ultimate insult for a Filipino is to be considered "*walang hiya*," or "without *hiya*," the unwelcome consequence of which is to lose the support of one's group.

The reverse side of the coin is *amor propio*, a sense of self, or self-respect. To offend someone's *amor propio* is to invite conflict. It is quite acceptable that if *amor propio* has been violated the balance must be redressed. In these instances fellow Filipinos will stand back to allow a new equilibrium to be established; however, this could involve violence and even loss of life.

Interwoven into the concept of face is *dangal*—self-respect based on what others think of one. It means that Filipinos can be trusted to do good work so that they will be well thought of by the boss. On the other hand, *dangal* also makes them very sensitive to being spoken to in a loud voice (synonymous with anger) and to public reprimands, which would give cause for great offense. Foreigners who naturally speak loudly should be careful lest they be perceived as angry, insulting, and arrogant.

It is important that you deal with those who work for you in a manner that does not offend them. The cardinal sin is to cause someone to lose face. There is no graver social *faux pas*. If a clerk forgets to give you an important message, you should accept the apology and suggest that in future a note should be put on your desk. The domestic helper who drops a crystal glass or plugs the 110-volt vacuum cleaner into the 220-volt outlet will be upset and apologetic. If you shout in these situations, your staff will lose face, your relationship will be spoiled, and their attitude to work may well deteriorate. Also, you should never call or refer to anyone as "stupid." It is considered to be extremely insulting.

Authority

The Philippines is a hierarchical society, and *paggalang*—respect for and deference to authority and one's elders—is part and parcel of it. The Filipino expects those in authority to be parent figures, and automatically accord them respect. A father's authority in the family is unchallenged, at least in public.

Anyone who is older than you should be called *Manang* or *Ate* (female) or *Manong* or *Kuya* (male), followed by their name, such as "*Manang* Sally." This is also a respectful form of address used between strangers.

People do not wish to intrude, and will bend their knees if they have to cross your path. Respectful behavior comes easily and naturally.

BAHALA NA

Underpinning the fabric of Filipino society is a deep belief in God. The Philippines is primarily a Roman Catholic country and God is very present in their worldview. *Bahala Na* is a value that articulates that belief. There is much debate, especially in academic circles, about its meaning and its impact on the behavior of the Filipinos. It literally means, "Leave it to God" (*Bahala* is the word for God).

In practical terms this has two results: an optimistic fatalism, where the individual feels resigned to the fact that life is in the lap of the gods and there is little one can do to influence outcomes; and an adventurousness and willingness to persevere in ambiguous or difficult circumstances. *Bahala Na* has given to many the capacity to cope both with poverty on a day-to-day basis, and the consequences of natural disasters. It brings hope to the hopeless; it is a coping mechanism for the vicissitudes of life. Many people have barely enough to live on, and yet there is very little resentment of the inequalities of life in the Philippines and the lack of opportunity for upward mobility.

Bahala Na, once invoked, puts into motion a psychology of courage, daring, and risk. A soldier said of the Filipinos that, "Apart from prayer, *Bahala Na* is their next most potent weapon in the field of combat and in times of crisis when all odds are against them."

MAÑANA—FILIPINO TIME

Mañana, of course, means "tomorrow," and reflects the attitude to time in the Philippines, where punctuality is not a priority. It has caused many an expatriate to tear his or her hair out while waiting for staff who casually saunter into a meeting fifteen minutes late, or for workmen who arrive three hours later than scheduled. It is true that traffic is bad and infrastructure is poor, and people may genuinely be late for these reasons; but "traffic" has become a very convenient excuse.

The Philippines is still an agricultural society at heart, in which time is seen as cyclical. Westerners view time as linear, and broken into precise units. Within a company setting, it is possible to insist on punctuality if it is very important to you. Some expatriate managers compromise by allowing up to ten minutes after the stipulated start time; others "fine" staff by having a charity box for latecomers. Foreigners are often advised to expect that a deadline will not be met, and, when planning, to make appropriate allowance.

If a report is needed by Friday, January 14, ask for it to be submitted on Monday, January 10. This will save you stress. If you expect a workman or a delivery to your home in the morning, it would be sensible to arrange to spend the day there.

Invited to a Filipino home? Don't be punctual. The host and hostess would be aghast if their guests arrived on time. The Filipinos attribute this to their Spanish colonial past, when etiquette demanded that the most important guest arrive last. President Estrada was known for being up to two hours late for official functions!

ATTITUDES TO FOREIGNERS

In general, Filipinos are very welcoming toward foreigners. Some people say that they still have a "colonial mentality," admiring fair skins and regarding imported goods as superior. There is also the stereotypical belief that all foreigners are very wealthy. For many Filipinos it would be a dream come true if they could go to live in the United States. Those who have done so often petition for their relations to join them.

Don't be surprised if Filipinos whom you have just met start asking you personal questions, for example about your marital status, your children, and how much rent you pay. This is how they try to establish a rapport and build a relationship with you. They don't intend to pry. If you don't feel comfortable, you don't need to be too specific with your answers. When asked about the rent, for example (many expatriates' houses cost more to rent than the monthly salary of the Filipino), just smile and say, "Too much!" They will understand that you do not want to discuss this further.

To those in the countryside, all white foreigners are American. Someone will probably come up to you and say, "Hi, Joe!"

MAKING THE RIGHT IMPRESSION

For a foreigner to function effectively, both professionally and personally, time and effort must be invested in building relationships. A friendly, smiling demeanor goes a long way toward this. The Filipinos are very helpful and hospitable people, and will go out of their way to make you feel welcome in their country.

If you are in a position of authority, remember that a firm but caring management style is one that resonates best with the Filipino. Most important of all, remember that there are different and valid ways of doing things, even if these may not be your usual ways.

chapter **three**

RELIGION & FESTIVALS

RELIGION

Religion is a vital aspect of the life of most Filipinos, who follow the teachings of the Catholic Church with the addition of some of their own practices. It reinforces their allegiance to the "kinship group," with the ceremonies relating to marriage, baptism, and death cementing the relationships within the group.

The Filipinos are a devout and tolerant people. Freedom of religion is a tenet of their Constitution, and this is respected. Nevertheless, as a result of three hundred years of Spanish occupation and missionary zeal, the country is predominantly Christian. It is estimated that the religious breakdown is: Catholic 85 percent; Protestant 5 percent; Christian cults 3 percent; Muslim 5 percent; others 2 percent.

In addition to traditional Catholics, there is a large charismatic Catholic group of over five million members, called El Shaddai. Their members are generally the poor, and over a million gather every week in a park beside Manila

Bay to listen to their leader, Brother Mike Velarde, who preaches in colloquial Tagalog. He recently lost some credibility due to his close involvement with Joseph Estrada. His influence, however, should not be underestimated; he is interested in politics and his followers are likely to vote according to his instructions.

The number of Protestants grew during the American period, and apart from the various traditional denominations there is a strong charismatic group, called The Jesus is Lord Fellowship, with over three million members. They are supportive of President GMA, and have close links with the U.S. televangelists.

In the past 110 years, two local Churches have sprung up. The Philippine Independent Church was founded by Gregorio Aglipay, a priest in the time of the rebellion against the Spanish, who left the Catholic Church. It has subsequently joined with the American Episcopalian Church. The Iglesia ni Cristo was founded in 1914 by Felix Manalo Ysagun. It builds huge churches of the same design throughout the country, is authoritarian, and requires its members to be clean, disciplined, and God-fearing.

Catholicism as practiced in the Philippines today basically follows official doctrine. Divorce is not permitted, but annulments can be obtained.

Children are taught the Catechism; adults attend Mass regularly, and in the office, it is quite normal to find employees reading their Bible. However, the pre-Hispanic animistic influence has blended in with Catholicism, resulting in a focus on the supernatural, and explains why there are so many followers of the charismatic groups.

> ### *SPIRITS ALL AROUND*
> At busy times in my office, my staff often had to work until 8:00 p.m. They were willing to do the overtime, but they were afraid to be there alone, because on several occasions they had seen a headless lady, dressed in white, walking through their work area.
>
> At home, our domestic helpers wanted us to call a priest to drive out an evil spirit that was disturbing their sleep at night. We obliged, and heard no more complaints. But ten years later, after we had moved to a new house, another helper commented that she now felt more relaxed because there was no evil spirit there.
>
> Whether you believe in the supernatural or not, it is necessary to listen to such concerns and take appropriate action, as far as possible, to allay fears. To ignore them would be insensitive and arrogant.

The inhabitants of Mindanao have been predominantly Muslim ("Moro") since the thirteenth century, and have fought for independence against the colonial powers and the Philippine government. They are generally zealous, strictly fasting during Ramadan, and many go on the *hajj*, the pilgrimage to Mecca. With financial support from overseas Islamic countries, many mosques and religious schools have been built. Women still enjoy a freedom not granted to them in fundamentalist countries.

The number of Christians in Mindanao increased under Marcos's resettlement program. This caused anger on the part of the Moros, since outsiders were taking away their land and natural resources. However, their anger is now directed more against the government, for the presence of the military, than against the Christian settlers.

CHRISTIAN FESTIVALS
Christmas

In the shops, the Christmas season starts in late September with the hanging of decorations and the playing of Christmas carols and songs in the malls. As Christmas draws closer, the decorations become more widespread and more extravagant. The Christmas atmosphere pervades the whole of Manila. The shops are packed, and traffic grinds to a standstill after work and all day Saturday.

In the residential areas, residents are expected to make a donation to the "village" for security, maintenance, and office personnel, and garbage collectors. A list may be issued indicating how much each resident contributed. Low-paid workers generally do a good job, and people do not begrudge them a little extra at Christmas. However, residents also find that they are greeted with a cheery and expectant "Merry Christmas!" by every service provider, from the mailman to the men who bring the utility bills. Sometimes an envelope is given to household staff to be passed on to the owner for filling!

Employees receive an extra month's salary at Christmas. They depend on this for all their extra expenses at this time, and it applies to both office and household staff. In the office, the staff working directly for you (or just your secretary if there are too many) also expect a gift, and they may give you a small present of food. Companies will give large gifts to good clients or customers. This is considered essential for business.

Everyone goes to Mass more frequently in the lead-up to Christmas, particularly in the early mornings. On Christmas Eve it is standing room only at the 10:00 p.m. Mass, and people go home for a feast of suckling pig and other delicacies.

The rest of the Christmas season is spent visiting or receiving family and friends. From Christmas Eve to the New Year offices are deserted, and it is not worth trying to make business appointments.

Lent

Filipino Catholics take Lent, or *Cuaresma*, very seriously, commencing with Mass on Ash Wednesday, when the sign of the cross is marked on their forehead. During Lent they may go to Mass more often, devote more time to prayer, fast, or give up small luxuries. Passion plays, which portray the life of Jesus, are performed throughout the country as the people prepare themselves for *Semana Santa* (Holy Week). *Semana Santa* takes place during the long school holidays, and Filipinos often return to their province to join their families. Many of those who stay in the city will take the whole week off work, and Maundy Thursday and Good Friday are public holidays.

Good Friday

On Good Friday in certain places, such as in Pampanga province, north of Manila, the crucifixion is reenacted. The participants flagellate themselves with whips consisting of sharp pieces of bamboo attached to string, causing the blood to flow. Others crawl on hands and knees. A crowd of devotees mixed with intrigued tourists follows the procession to the crucifixion site. The hands of the person portraying Jesus may be nailed briefly or bound to the cross as the hot sun beats down. The Catholic Church does not encourage this practice, but in the Philippines religion combines the standard teachings with its own traditions. In this case, the reenactment arose from the sufferings of the Filipino people during Spanish rule. Thus, they believed they could identify closely with the sufferings of Jesus, who did not deserve such treatment. Today a similar attitude to suffering enables the poor to deal with their poverty.

Easter Sunday

On Easter Sunday, there is joyful celebration of the resurrection of Jesus. Expatriates hold a sunrise service at the American cemetery, and churches are full of worshipers. In some towns the *salubong* ceremony is performed: in procession, men and boys follow an image of Jesus while women and girls follow an image of Mary, mother of Jesus, until the two groups meet in the church.

The blend of Christianity and folklore becomes most apparent in the *moriones* legend of

Longinus, which is reenacted in Marinduque, an island off Batangas province in Luzon. The *moriones* were Roman soldiers from the time of Jesus, and the participants wear appropriate masks. During Holy Week they wander around the town and join in the various processions. On Easter Sunday one of them, Longinus, who was assigned to watch the tomb of Jesus, declares that Christ has risen from the dead. The other *moriones* turn against him and, although he escapes at first, they arrest him and, after he has affirmed his faith, behead him.

The cynical may comment that such events are continued for financial reasons, since they attract visitors. However, traditions die hard in the Philippines, especially when they promote community spirit, provide the opportunity for a celebration, and portray piety. On the other hand, wealthier urban dwellers take advantage of the long weekend by going to their own province, or to the hills or the beach. The roads are crowded as everyone returns to Manila on Easter Sunday.

All Saints' Day

November 1, All Saints' Day, is a public holiday, and a time to remember loved ones who have passed away. It is taken seriously, but is not a very somber occasion. It is an opportunity for a get-together. Families go to the cemeteries, put up tents, have picnics, and play cards. Stalls sell food and drink to the crowds, and parking places can be hard to find. Unless you are going to a cemetery yourself, it is wiser to stay off the roads.

FIESTAS

The Filipinos are fun-loving people, and this is illustrated by the various *fiestas* that are celebrated in towns and villages throughout the country, particularly during May, the hottest month of the year, when the children are on holiday. A *fiesta* may commemorate a religious or historical event, be based on a traditional ritual, or combine these themes together. It may be a thanksgiving celebration for a plentiful harvest, or honor the patron saint of the town. *Fiestas* may involve parades of floats on the river, *carabao* (water buffalo) festivals, flower festivals, rain dances, ethnic sports events, and more, and are frequently combined with commemorative Masses for a patron saint or for the Virgin Mary.

It is inappropriate for outsiders to be critical of the pagan aspect of these Christian acts of worship. The uniqueness of the Catholicism of Filipinos and their ability to enjoy themselves, despite poverty, is wholly admirable.

Each *barangay* had its own *fiesta*. In the cities the importance of the *fiesta* has declined, but in the countryside it retains its social importance.

Those who are away from their villages return with gifts for their families and old friends, and show how successful they have been. This can be expensive, and low-paid workers may have mixed emotions about returning for the *fiesta*.

Town centers are cleaned, houses are spruced up, and brightly colored decorations are hung along the streets. Everyone is involved in some way with processions, music, games, sideshows, and food. Special dishes, such as *lechon* (roast pig), are prepared, even though the cost may stretch the family budget. The hospitable nature of Filipinos is evident, as villagers wander from house to house talking and eating. Strangers are welcomed. If you join in a village *fiesta*, however, make sure that you show respect for any images, such as those of patron saints and Santo Niño, as they are carried through the streets .

Despite the hard work of the community, a *fiesta* involves considerable financial outlay. The wealthy and influential pay for particular items, and in this way gain useful prestige. All donations are welcome, and as you drive through a village just before its *fiesta*, you may find some children holding a piece of string across the road to stop you. They will ask you for a donation for the *fiesta*. Give something—they will be happy.

The three *fiestas* described below have become famous, and are sometimes referred to as the "Mardi Gras" of the Philippines, though this is a reference to the style of the fiesta rather than the religious aspect, as they all take place in January.

Ati-Atihan

Ati-Atihan means "acting like the Ati." Ati is the original name for the early inhabitants of the Philippines, the Negritos, who were dark-skinned with curly hair. In the thirteenth century, a group of Malay settlers reached the shores of Panay Island in the Western Visayas, which was then heavily populated by the Ati. In

order to allay the concerns of the Ati, the settlers imitated their hosts, and painted their faces with soot to look like them. Therefore, the *Ati-Atihan* festival participants put soot on their skin and leaves in their hair, and dress in suitable costumes.

Musicians and dancers parade through the streets, dancing and beating their drums in a simple rhythm. This parade also brings in a religious theme, as the Cross and a statue representing the baby Jesus are carried around the village square, and everyone shouts "*Viva Santo Niño!*," in memory of the Christ Child.

The largest *Ati-Atihan* festival is celebrated on Panay Island, in the town of Kalibo, in the third week of January. The festival attracts a huge number of visitors, and has become very commercialized. Everybody dresses up, and the visitors join the local musicians and dancers. There is a captivating atmosphere of color, sound, movement, and excitement.

Dinagyang

Dinagyang means "to make merry," and this is the theme of the *fiesta* that is held on the fourth weekend of January in Iloilo, on the opposite side of the island of Panay from Kalibo. The Iloilo festival started in 1968 after a replica of the statue of Santo Niño was brought there, and the first street festival was held in 1976. It has now become very popular. The focus is on a competition between dance groups, and although the onlookers do not participate as they do in Kalibo, plenty of fun is guaranteed.

Sinulog

This festival is held in Cebu, the largest city in the Visayas, for ten days in mid-January. It blends the history of Cebu with homage to the Santo Niño.

When Magellan landed in the Philippines in 1521, he gave a statue of the Christ Child to the chief of the tribe, who was baptized into the

Christian faith. When the Spanish returned in 1565, after Magellan's death, they noticed that the statue had been placed with those of other gods and that homage was paid to them all every year. The other statues were removed and the religious ritual was retained solely for the Santo Niño.

The purely religious aspect was expanded into a festival in 1980. A historical presentation links the pagan past and the Christianity of the present brought by the Spanish. Floats represent the different periods of history, and participants wear costumes to match those periods. Battles are reenacted, Miss Cebu is crowned, there are concerts and competitions, food and drink. Most important of all, Mass is celebrated and the statue of Santo Niño is paraded through the streets.

ISLAMIC FESTIVALS

Devout Muslims fast for a month in Ramadan; they do not eat or drink from sunrise to sunset. Owing to hunger and the possibility of dehydration, productivity may be affected during this period. The end of Ramadan is celebrated by *Eid-al-Fitr*, or *Hari-Raya Puasa*. On this day, Muslims go through ritual cleansing and attend congregational prayer at the mosques. This is followed by festivities, with plenty to eat as the day focuses on generosity and charity.

A second festival is *Eid-al-Adzha*, or *Hari-Raya Hadji*. This is a day of sacrifice to Allah, and a sheep or goat will be killed and distributed to relatives, neighbors, and the poor. It is also a day of prayer and forgiveness.

OTHER CELEBRATIONS

Filipinos don't need an excuse to have a party, but they welcome the opportunity to celebrate a variety of occasions, a number of which have come through American influence.

At New Year's, fireworks are let off throughout the country, particularly on New Year's Eve, but also throughout the Christmas/New Year's season. Be on your guard against the nuisance and danger of inferior fireworks, and firecrackers thrown into roads. Guns are often fired into the air, and of course accidents happen; the government is trying to put a stop to this practice.

Filipinos consider themselves to be *macho*, and Filipinas believe in romance. Thus, in the cities Valentine's Day is a perfect day for those who can afford it to enjoy a romantic celebration at a restaurant. The less romantic are advised to stay at home because the traffic is gridlocked.

Halloween gives children an opportunity to dress up as ghosts or monsters and go from house to house "trick or treating."

chapter **four**

THE FILIPINOS AT HOME

HOUSING

The quality of housing in Manila ranges from the vast and extravagant houses of the rich and famous to the wood, cardboard, and even paper huts put up by the poor and unemployed. Until a recent cleanup of the area, thousands of people lived off the refuse dump known as Smokey Mountain. In many areas proper sanitation is nonexistent, and untreated sewage and refuse go directly into the rivers.

Boxes for Houses

As we unpacked our shipment of personal effects in Manila, we wondered what to do with all the packing materials. We needn't have worried. The landlord's gardener came and asked if he could have it all—wood, paper, and cardboard. His friend who drove a jeepney would help him with the transportation. They needed the materials to strengthen their houses, and to add "wallpaper."

Well-off Filipinos in Metro Manila generally live in "villages," apartments, or family compounds. "Villages" are gated residential areas, where the land has been divided into lots. The purchasers of a lot build a house on it to suit their needs. Each village is managed by a village association, with a voluntary residents' committee. Residents pay dues, and the association organizes maintenance and security. Most villages are surrounded by a wall, with controlled gates and security guards.

As evidence of economic growth, the number of high-rise buildings (both residential and office) has increased dramatically over the past fifteen years. This can be seen most clearly in the skyline of Makati and the newer areas of Manila, such as Ortigas and Fort Bonifacio. Large, luxurious apartments in Makati enable executives to get to work in just a few minutes, while the open space in Fort Bonifacio makes it worthwhile spending ten minutes for the short car journey to Makati. Security is tight in these apartment buildings.

Some wealthy Filipinos live in family compounds. In traditional families children are not expected to move out when they grow up. When a son marries, his wife joins his family. Space and finance permitting, a separate house is built for the couple within the compound. With security being an issue of concern, particularly to the Chinese Filipinos, the family compounds are surrounded by high walls, and security guards are on duty round the clock.

Some middle-class Filipinos live in "subdivisions," which have smaller lots and less security than the more expensive villages. Others live in townhouses or apartments located outside the Makati Central Business District. Despite transportation difficulties, many can only afford to live in the suburbs, and therefore spend a lot of time traveling between home and work.

In rural areas, wealthy people live in concrete structures, and the rest in bamboo huts with palm frond roofs.

Renting

When renting a house or apartment, it is common practice for a year's rent to be paid in advance, plus one or two months' rental as a deposit. The extent of maintenance and repairs undertaken by the landlord during the tenancy depends not so much on the contract as on the landlord-tenant relationship. As with most nationalities, there are excellent landlords, who will respond immediately to your requests for repairs and with whom you can establish a good relationship, and there are those who are interested only in the money.

House Blessing

When Catholic Filipinos move into a new house they and their friends celebrate the occasion with a House Blessing. The priest says prayers and sprinkles holy water in all corners of the house, and the image of the family's patron saint may be enshrined. Then the guests, enjoying a wide variety of food prepared for the occasion, wish prosperity on the house owners. With the blessing of God and the support of their friends, the owners hope that their house will become a true home, attended by happiness and prosperity.

DAILY LIFE AND ROUTINES

One of the major concerns of the Filipinos living in Metro Manila is the traffic congestion. Whereas the British are said to talk endlessly about the weather, with Filipinos it is the traffic! Either because they live far away from the city where there is no commuter train service, or in order to minimize the time spent on the road, or both, many Filipinos leave home as early as 5:30 a.m. By 7:00 a.m., traffic is already building up. Some skip an early breakfast and have something to eat on arrival at the office or worksite, if there is a cafeteria; there is also a mid morning break for *merienda* (a snack).

The well-off, who live nearer to the city, have a driver to take them to the office. Some of those who live further out of town may have their own helicopter, which can land on the roofs of various buildings in the city.

The lunch hour is normally from 12:00 noon to 1:00 p.m. Since breakfast may have been eaten at 5:00 a.m., with only *merienda* in between, most people are hungry by then. If you want lunch in a shopping mall at 12:30 p.m. you will be lucky to find a table, and there will be long lines in the food halls. These consist of a variety of stalls, usually in the basement but still air-conditioned, selling Filipino dishes, fast food of many kinds, desserts, fruit, and drinks. After lunch, office workers may take a little *siesta*, resting their heads on their desk. Those working out of doors stretch out on the ground. For them the midday heat is truly exhausting, particularly after the early start.

Executives may have lunch with clients. Relationships are of primary importance, so the opportunity to socialize must always be taken, and a meal must never be rushed.

As soon as work ends, the long journey home begins. If overtime is necessary in order to complete an urgent piece of work, this is readily accepted, since it provides additional money and usually means slightly less time on the road, assuming work continues until after 7:00 p.m.

At home, there are household chores to be done (usually by the women!), time is spent with the children, and an early night is taken in preparation for the next morning's early start.

THE FAMILY AND CHILDREN

The importance of the family is recognized in the 1987 Constitution: "The State recognizes the Filipino family as the foundation of the nation. Accordingly it shall strengthen its solidarity and promote its total development." In order to strengthen the family, marriage is regarded as "an inviolable social institution," and the family has the right to a "family living wage and income."

Within the family, children are extremely important. Many Filipinos still have large families, and like to have children of both sexes. They are generally very indulgent toward the small children: discipline comes later. Babies and toddlers are kissed, cuddled, carried, and given attention that would be impossible without an extended family. With the mother at work, grandparents often take responsibility for child care. Alternatively, a maid is recruited—often a teenage cousin, or a daughter of friends, coming to Manila for the first time. Most young Filipinas love babies, probably because they themselves have grown up in a large extended family and are used to having them around. Foreigners should not be surprised if a Filipina waitress or sales assistant picks up or touches their baby.

Babies are never left alone, and their *yaya* (nursemaid) sleeps in the same room. Many foreigners tell the *yaya* that the baby can sleep alone while she does other things; but this may make her anxious.

Don't Leave Him Alone!
One day a woman entered our house by the back door, searched the bedrooms, and found my wife's jewelry. On her way downstairs she met our son's *yaya*. She said "I'm Doctora Abad. Why have you left the baby alone in his room?" Our *yaya* ran to the bedroom, and the con woman disappeared with the jewelry.

In most families, parents begin to discipline their children when they reach school age. The children are then required to help with household chores, including looking after younger siblings. Since education is regarded as vital for future success, schoolwork is taken seriously.

Children are taught respect for their elders, politeness, social sensitivity, patience, and obedience. Aggression between siblings is dealt with strictly, to maintain harmony and cooperation within the family. A common way of disciplining children is to tease them, because this conveys one's views on their behavior while avoiding direct criticism. As a result of their upbringing, Filipino children are generally well-behaved and polite; but in some wealthy families the overindulgence of babyhood continues, resulting in spoiled children who order the staff around and never do anything for themselves.

Teenagers go around with their *barkada* (peer group), and although boy-girl relationships may develop, the focus is generally on the group. A girl's eighteenth birthday is a special occasion. If her family is wealthy, she has a debutante ball at a hotel—a formal affair, with tuxedos and ball gowns, to which family and friends are invited.

A young Filipina would not lightly marry against the wishes of her family. A marriage is the joining of two families rather than just two individuals, and a couple will ask parents and grandparents for advice on difficult issues.

Respect and appreciation for older people is such that time will be spent with them by younger family members, even when minds and bodies are no longer alert. It is the responsibility of the family to look after its older members, and this is endorsed by the 1987 Constitution: "The family has the duty to care for its elderly members but the State may also do so through just programs of social justice."

Socializing

In wealthy families the wife may not work, but will spend her time organizing her domestic staff, going to the gym, meeting friends, and involving herself in community or charity work. In the evenings she goes with her husband to any event to which they have been invited. The Filipinos are sociable people, and in Manila there are a great many functions. Diplomats find that this is one of their most active and enjoyable postings—but they keep quiet about this, so that there is no objection to their request for an extension!

For the less wealthy, time, exhaustion, and the family set a limit on social activity. But when they do go out, they enjoy themselves in Church activities, sports, or karaoke.

FAMILY CELEBRATIONS
Weddings
Among the upper and middle classes, weddings are celebrated in style. Huge amounts of money are spent on the wedding dress, church

decorations, and a reception for many guests. Most are sponsored by a third party.

Wedding sponsors are chosen on the basis of their social position. These could be prominent politicians, successful businessmen, or company executives. The primary sponsors may be regarded as godparents to the couple, and in Filipino culture this brings responsibilities relating to assistance in their careers, if necessary. To be asked to be a main sponsor is a great honor. There may be a number of other sponsors at a wedding, such as candle or veil sponsors, who are generally family or friends; they each have a specific duty to perform.

The wedding ceremony follows the pattern of any Western Catholic Church, with the couple making their vows, the priest giving a short homily, and the signing of the register. After the ceremony a reception is given at a restaurant or private club by the families of the bride and groom. They have invited more friends to this, and the number of guests escalates considerably. On the way in there is a table on which the guests place their gifts before being greeted by the bride and groom. There are photographs, a sumptuous meal, cake cutting, and, if the bride and groom are Westernized, speeches.

It all seems rather like a Western wedding, but there is an important social difference. This is not a marriage of two individuals: it is a marriage of two families. There are to be no mother-in-law jokes! Family bonds are forged through marriage, and there are certain responsibilities, of which some Western men who marry Filipinas are unaware. If a husband is wealthy, and his wife's family is not, he will be expected to provide for them financially; and the expatriate executive will be expected to find employment for relatives. Unless this is understood in advance, the marriage is unlikely to be harmonious.

Baptisms

Infant baptism is an important ceremony for Filipinos, not so much for religious reasons as for the fact that godfather (*ninong*) and godmother (*ninang*) are brought into a special relationship with the child. Godparents are expected to do more than give presents. They are expected to act as second parents, giving advice and assistance to their godchild. This could come in the form of material help or, at a later date, in getting a job. The parents and godparents will become closer than mere friends; they will be regarded as family, and *compadres*.

When a Westerner is invited to be a godparent, the invitation should be accepted as an honor. At the same time, the parents of the child will be held in high esteem for being in a position to have a Westerner as a godparent. A foreigner's responsibilities would generally be limited to attending the baptism and the giving of a generous gift. A lifelong relationship with the child would be expected of a close friend, but not of the boss.

Funerals

When anyone within the extended family dies, the survivors enter a period of mourning. Family ties are close, and grief is genuine. A wake, which may last several days before the funeral, is held for family, friends, and acquaintances, and going to this is more important than attending the funeral. If a parent or spouse of a member of staff has died, the boss should go to the wake.

The wake may take place in a private room in the church or, particularly in the case of those who cannot afford that, at home. The carefully prepared body is placed in an open coffin. On arrival there will be a book to be signed by all those who have attended. Look for the bereaved, express your condolences, go to the open coffin, and pay your respects. You will be offered a drink. Despite the grief, the opportunity to socialize is never lost. The cost of a wake and funeral is considerable, and a company may help an employee with this in the event of the death of a close relative. An envelope is often passed around the office so that colleagues can make a contribution to the expenses or for flowers.

The piety of Filipinos is such that, together with the natural sense of loss attendant on a death, there is also a deep belief in the life hereafter.

ENTERTAINING

If you invite a Filipino friend to dinner, he may not come, even if he said he would be free. You should repeat the invitation a couple of days before the dinner, so that he is quite certain that you really want him to attend. Even then, if he is unable or unwilling to come, he is unlikely to turn down the invitation to your face, preferring to do so through a third party. If you send a written invitation, it is unlikely that he will accept in writing. If he does so he will feel under a greater obligation to attend.

Before business functions, secretaries spend a great deal of time on the telephone, trying to find out who is intending to come. Even at this stage a positive response does not guarantee attendance. If a VIP, such as a cabinet secretary, is the honored guest, attendance will be much better.

Most business entertaining is carried out in clubs or restaurants. You are expected to enjoy the food and drink; but never eat and drink to excess. Loss of control is regarded as shameful. Many women consume only soft drinks—it is the men who drink in Filipino society. There may be singing after the meal, and, if you join in, it will be well received even if you are a little off-key!

If you are invited to a Filipino home for dinner, do not arrive punctually. This would imply that you were anxious for social acceptance, or eager to eat the meal. It is preferable to arrive as much as half an hour late, and to behave with reticence. When it is suggested that you sit down at the table, or help yourself to a buffet-style dinner, don't immediately do so; wait to be asked again. This is not annoying for the host or hostess, but a feature of Filipino etiquette.

Take care when complimenting the hostess on the excellent food. A quick compliment is fine, but don't overdo it unless you are sure that she actually made it herself, because wealthy Filipinos all have cooks! Find something else to praise, such as the flower arrangements or the décor, for which she will have been responsible.

At the end of the meal, leave a little food on your plate to signify that you have been fully satisfied by your host's generosity. Keep some space for dessert—a part of the meal greatly enjoyed by Filipinos. If you are giving a party, remember that this course is important.

During the meal, conversation will not be a problem because educated Filipinos speak good English. If you are on a long visit, they will naturally want to know how you are settling down in the country. Do not take this as an opportunity to complain about inefficiencies or to criticize the government or the people, or you will be regarded as arrogant. Always be polite and self-effacing. You could ask general questions that will contribute to your understanding of life in the Philippines, or ask advice on certain matters that you are finding difficult to understand in a new culture. On the other hand, don't be surprised if you are asked unusually personal questions. The intention is to understand your background.

At the end of the evening, guests may be given leftover food to take home. This is an old tradition, called *pabaon*. If there are grandparents at the dinner, it is, of course, polite to say good-bye to them as well as to your host and hostess.

Gifts

When you are invited to dinner at a Filipino home, a gift is not expected, but if you do take one it will be welcomed. Do not take food or wine to more traditional Filipinos—this may look to them as though you think they might not have provided adequately for the occasion. However, among Westernized Filipinos such gifts are unlikely to cause offense.

If it is a birthday party, you should take a present. It will not be opened in front of you; it will be put to one side to be opened later. There are two reasons for this: first, the giver would be embarrassed if the gift were of less monetary value than those brought by other guests; second, it is considered materialistic to open a present the moment it is received. The recipient may thank you for it the next time you meet, and will know exactly what it was, even if your name was not attached to it. Similarly, you should not open in public any presents that are given to you.

HOUSEHOLD HELP

Household help is a unique feature of domestic life in the Philippines, and one that visiting Westerners should be aware of. In the past, many household helpers worked all their lives for one family. They became so attached to their employers that their honesty and dependability were guaranteed, and children could be left in their care in the knowledge that they would risk their lives for the safety of their charges. In return, the employers would treat them well, helping their families in an emergency, contributing toward the education of their children, and ensuring that they had a roof over their heads all their lives. Often, their children were offered an "apprenticeship" within the household.

Life is not bad for helpers in wealthy Filipino families; they talk and joke together and are never lonely. In addition, there is more space, with large houses having maids' quarters. Foreigners often employ two helpers to avoid having one lonely one. If the two are related, or at least come from the same province and speak the same language, the chances that they will get along well together are greater.

It is generally accepted that Filipino employers pay lower wages than foreigners, but that they are also more prepared to become involved in the personal lives of their domestic staff. Employment is often terminated when the foreigner leaves the country, although many foreigners take their household help on to their next assignment.

Household helpers realize that working for foreigners is better paid, but know that they need to speak English to get such a job. However, since it is not easy to find a reliable helper who speaks good English, those that do can be selective in their choice of employer. There is clear racial bias, with the preference being for "white" foreigners (Americans, English, Australians, Europeans), who are seen as more generous and less demanding than other Asians.

Filipinos are generally strict with their household staff, and may give them only one day off every two weeks. Working hours are long, starting early with the preparation of breakfast and perhaps ending only when the employer wants nothing more to eat or drink. The *yaya* (nursemaid) sleeps with the child in her care and is responsible for him or her all the time.

Some foreigners, on the other hand, become too lax and friendly toward the helpers by inviting them to eat or watch TV with the family. The helpers normally prefer to eat and relax on their own, and find such invitations embarrassing. The danger for the employers is that the relationship is blurred, with the Filipina coming to regard them as friends and seeing nothing wrong in taking advantage of their generosity. When choosing helpers, the better workers are often those who come directly from working for Filipino families and who have not been confused or spoiled by white foreigners.

There is a hierarchy within the household helpers beyond that of mere age. The cook is considered to be at the top because she is in charge of the food. Next comes the *yaya,* followed by the house girl, who is in charge of cleaning and/or washing. In some households there is a *lavandera*, a laundress. A helper might also describe herself as "all around"—this means she can do some cooking and the washing and ironing, and will keep an eye on the children. Most foreigners prefer to hire "all arounds" rather than follow the strict hierarchy of a Filipino household.

If you have a driver, there are a few extra points to remember. Make sure, when you give him an instruction or send him on an errand, that he understands exactly what he has to do. If you ask, "Do you understand?" he will answer, "Yes," even if he doesn't. He gains status from the fact that he is in charge of the most expensive piece of equipment that you own—the car. He will not take instructions from the female helpers (except possibly the cook, because otherwise she may refuse to feed him!), but only from you, so you must ensure that you understand each other.

The first reaction of a driver who is involved in a traffic accident may well be laughter. He is not laughing because he thinks it is funny; he is doing so because he is worried and frightened.

Drivers have to be watched carefully, because, although they may have a wife and six children, they may also have a wandering eye for the girls, and this can lead to trouble in the household.

Emergency Loans

As a rich foreigner, you will probably be asked for a loan at some time. Family emergencies arise, inevitably, and you, as the employer, are seen as a source of assistance. If the need appears genuine, such as a medical emergency, the inclination is to help. However, unless the person has worked well for you for some time and you know his or her character, you could be taken for a ride. Even if repayment is promised according to an agreed schedule, you must be prepared to face the fact that it may not happen. You might need to waive some of the loan, if an effort has clearly been made. Even an honest helper might disappear rather than face the embarrassment of failing to make the repayments.

Having household helpers and a driver, a gardener, and a swimming pool serviceman is the norm for wealthy Filipinos and well-paid foreigners. How they are selected and managed determines whether they are a source of assistance or frustration. Filipino families establish clear ground rules and an appropriate employer/employee relationship, in which they treat their staff well in return for good work. All staff, at the beginning of employment, should be given clear guidelines, so that they know exactly what is expected of them and what they may not do.

chapter **five**

TIME OUT

Since the Philippines is a relationship-based society, Filipinos do not spend all their waking hours in the office. They will work overtime because they need the extra money, but leisure time with family and friends is very important. How do they spend this time?

SHOPPING

Shopping is a popular pastime at most levels of urban society. There are huge shopping malls in Manila, and at weekends they teem with people. Normally they open from around 10:00 a.m. until 9.30 p.m. every day of the week. When payday falls on a Friday the malls have an evening of "Midnight Madness," with special offers on cheaper goods. On such evenings there are appalling traffic jams around the malls. The malls that are further away from public transportation are generally more expensive, with more designer shops and upscale restaurants. Nevertheless, they too are crowded on weekends.

A particular attraction of the shopping malls is the fact that they are air-conditioned. Those who do not have air-conditioning at home—and these are the majority of Filipinos—relax in the cool environment, look around the shops, watch a movie, and have a meal.

SPORTS AND GAMES

Sports are an important aspect of life for many Filipinos. The national sport is basketball. Most people have a television set, and enthusiastically watch the basketball matches. Opportunities to play most sports are limited, but basketball can be played in the street.

Basketball

The question many expatriates ask is, "Why do all Filipino males play basketball, when most of them are not very tall? Why don't they choose a sport which is more suitable for their size?" One answer to this question is the American influence, and the fact that there is so much TV coverage of both U.S. and Philippine basketball. However, more important is the fact that basketball requires little space and no expensive equipment. In comparison with soccer and American football, basketball is played in a small area, either under cover or in the open air. Thus, it can be played throughout the year, even during the rainy season.

All rural villages have a concrete basketball court. Once it is built, maintenance is minimal and the cost of balls is low. In a poor neighborhood, a hoop is erected in the street for the local boys to have fun and practice their skills. Thus, for reasons of space (in Manila) and cost, no other sport could be played by so many Filipinos. Within the teams there is a strong team spirit, and a great determination to win.

The Philippines has its own professional basketball league, which is boosted by the presence of imports from the U.S., thanks to sponsorship by big companies such as Shell or San Miguel, and the quality of play is quite high. Supporters are fervent, and tickets for matches are generally sold out in advance. But if you can't get a ticket, you will still be able to watch it on TV!

Golf

The number of golf clubs has increased dramatically over the past ten years. The most prestigious club in Manila is Manila Golf, which occupies prime land between Makati and Fort Bonifacio. The cost of transferable membership fell from P50 million before the Asian financial crisis in 1997 to about P25 million in 2003. The value of the land accounts for the high price, and so some members are only speculators, not players. The players are able to tee off at 6:00 a.m., play nine holes, have breakfast, and be in the office by 9:00 a.m.

Some new golf courses built outside Manila are magnificent, especially those in Tagaytay, ninety minutes' drive away, about 1,640 feet (500 meters) above sea level and overlooking a volcanic lake. But beware of buying a share in a course under construction: it may never be finished!

For businessmen, golf has become a very important game. Business relationships are formed and cemented on the golf course, and an invitation to play a round on a working Friday afternoon should not be turned down lightly.

Soccer

The Philippines participates in international soccer competitions, such as the World Cup preliminaries, but their performances have been disappointing. Soccer is played at all the private Filipino schools in Manila, some of which have huge grounds with up to ten pitches. Through sponsorship, more soccer is also being played in rural areas. However, the long-term benefits have not yet materialized. Talented sportsmen from poorer backgrounds choose basketball, because that is where the money is. The wealthy and well educated go into business, playing soccer merely for fun.

One of the best weekends of the year is a six-a-side mini World Cup soccer competition organized by expatriates. The enthusiasm and emotions run high, as the players (from sixteen to sixty years old!) represent their own country. The Filipino team, always with a number of Spanish *mestizos*, generally performs very creditably, often reaching the final.

Bowling

Ten-pin bowling attracts a considerable following in Manila. It is not surprising that the Philippines boasts a world champion, because even if one's office does not have a team, bowling invariably features in social events. More important than being a good bowler and winning is the willingness to take part and be part of the group.

Pool

Pool is another sport at which the Philippines has a world champion, and the large number of pool halls provides opportunities for many to participate.

Chess

Chess is played by all sectors of society, not only by the educated and intellectual. Security guards assigned to protect the houses and families of the rich will often pass the time playing chess. The Philippines has performed well in international chess competitions for many years, and used to hold the presidency of the International Chess Federation. However, conflict between two groups recently led to an attempt to enter two national teams in an international competition. In fact, sports at the highest level are often undermined by rival administrators and politicians, who compete to head the sports council or a particular sport. The benefits of a high-level position relate most obviously to travel for overseas competitions, including the Olympics.

Sports Clubs

There are a number of sports clubs in Manila, none of which are cheap to join. The most expensive is the Manila Polo Club, which in addition to polo offers activities including tennis, swimming, baseball, squash, and show jumping, and a golf driving range. As for the polo, it is a rich man's sport, but the quality of both horses and riders provides an enjoyable Sunday afternoon's entertainment. Multinational companies often give Polo Club membership to senior executives, but they are advised to enjoy the sporting activities and avoid the club politics.

GAMBLING

Gambling is prevalent in the Philippines, as in many other countries. It is alleged that President Estrada would stay up into the early hours of the morning playing cards; he would not start work until noon at the earliest. Unfortunately, the poor are as addicted to gambling as the rich.

> ### *GAMBLING AND SELF-DESTRUCTION*
> Newly arrived in the Philippines, I needed to buy some furniture for my house. A friend recommended a good cane furniture maker, who agreed to deliver what I wanted within three weeks. I paid him a deposit of 50 percent. Three weeks later I asked him how he was progressing. "A little delay; another two weeks." Two weeks later he told me he had finished the job, but that he couldn't deliver for another week as his truck was being repaired. A week later, he had to go away to look after his sick mother.
>
> In despair, I contacted my friend, who undertook to help. He himself had previously lent the man money for his business. I soon learned that the man had disappeared. He had gambled away my deposit, had borrowed more money, and had lost that too. He was now in debt, and afraid to remain in Manila.

Cockfighting is popular. Huge crowds gather to place bets, and owners spend large amounts of money and effort on training their birds.

One of the most infamous illegal gambling games is *jueteng*. This is a lottery-style game, in which punters choose a two-number combination between one and thirty-seven. Police and town officials have been paid to turn a blind eye, while the operators make huge profits, primarily at the expense of the poor, who are the main participants. The kickbacks from the operators are alleged to have reached the former president Estrada, and this led to his downfall. With the support of the new government and the Catholic Church, strenuous attempts have been made to put a stop to *jueteng*.

Legal lotteries now provide another form of gambling, the attraction of which is understandable in so poor a country.

NIGHTLIFE

The Philippines is renowned for its "girlie" bars, and although these continue to attract expatriates and locals alike, it is unfortunate that this is the image of Manila that is often presented to the world. There is far more to nightlife in Manila!

The Filipinos have a wide range of artistic

talents, and this is paraded in a variety of settings. Acting and music come naturally, and you should not miss the opportunity to go to a musical, especially if Lea Salonga is in the cast. Both in London's West End and on Broadway, many of the lead performers and chorus for the original *Miss Saigon* were Filipinos. Imelda Marcos recognized such talent and was responsible for the construction of the Cultural Center of the Philippines. Concerts and plays of the highest quality are now performed, there and elsewhere.

Excellent singing and dancing can also be enjoyed in the cultural shows put on for tourists. These are a mixture of pre-Spanish and Spanish music and dance. The music may be played on gongs and bamboo flutes (pre-Spanish) and the guitar (Spanish), and the dancing may include vigorous and rhythmic pre-Spanish dances, flamenco, and elegant Spanish dances. The shows end with audience participation in *Tinikling*, regarded as the Philippine national dance. Imitating the movement of the *tikling* birds in the fields, the dancers step between bamboo poles, which are moved around on the ground and knocked against each other. The music speeds up, the poles are moved faster, and the dancers have to keep in rhythm, or their ankles will suffer!

A recent craze in Manila, especially for the rich, is ballroom dancing. Their menfolk absent, either working or not interested, the women dance with instructors (DIs)—often students who need to make some money to see them through university. There have been some stories of women becoming attached to these young men, and handing over a fortune!

Performing

Karaoke and videoke are very popular. One of my staff owned a bar, which made little profit until he invested in a karaoke machine. He quickly recouped the cost and was able to open a second bar.

FOOD AND DRINK

The sociable and friendly Filipinos enjoy eating together, and although the food may be of less interest than the company, it does play an important part. The staple food is rice, which may be eaten at every meal, accompanied by meat, fish, vegetables, or, for the poor, dried fish. Extra flavor is provided by coconut, soy, and vinegar.

Filipino food, like Filipino culture, has various influences, particularly Malay, Chinese, and Spanish. The Malay influence is particularly strong in Muslim Mindanao, which resisted Spanish attempts at occupation. Thus, the food in Mindanao is much spicier, with greater use of coconut milk and no pork. It is estimated that about 80 percent of the dishes outside Mindanao are derived from Spanish or Mexican cuisine. Two popular dishes are chicken or pork *adobo*, which is cooked in vinegar and soy, and *lechon*, roast suckling pig, whose crackling is much tastier than the fat under it, provided you don't have brittle teeth. Fish is a major feature, but fresh fish is easier to get outside Manila due to the polluted waters of Manila Bay. Another popular dish is *pancit*, the Filipino version of Chinese noodles, mixed with meat and vegetables.

Local fruits such as mango, melon, and papaya provide an excellent finale. *Halo-halo* is a dessert consisting of layers of preserved or sweetened fruit, gelatin, custard, and crushed ice, sometimes topped by a scoop of ice cream. In fact, ice cream seems to be appreciated at any time of the day!

You may also be introduced to the famous aphrodisiac *balut*—a half-formed duck embryo, which is eaten whole, including beak and feathers. Filipinos realize that this is an acquired taste, and will offer it to foreigners with a smile and little expectation that they will be taken up on it.

The cities have a range of Western and Asian restaurants, many of which prepare fine food at reasonable prices. Also, pasta and fast food with French fries are becoming increasingly popular.

As regards drink, beer, especially the very good local San Miguel, is widely consumed throughout the Philippines. Carbonated soft drinks are also very popular. As an alternative to soft drinks, fresh *buko*, or coconut juice, is most refreshing on a hot day, and iced tea is often drunk with meals.

Table Manners

The Filipinos are likely to bow their heads in thanks or to cross themselves before eating.

A spoon is generally held in the right hand and a fork in the left. A knife is used where necessary, and will be provided in a good restaurant. In rural areas, and among the poor urban workers, rice is eaten with the hands. Some city restaurants that cater to tourists offer the option of the *kamayan* style of eating, with the hands, off a banana leaf instead of a plate.

chapter six

TRAVEL, HEALTH, & SAFETY

ROAD TRAVEL AND TRANSPORTATION
Cars

Returning from a weekend at the beach, you may find yourself in a traffic jam all the way to the town ahead. Vehicles attempt to overtake on both sides, lining up all over the road and off it, on the inside, and on the side on which cars are coming from the opposite direction! The oncoming vehicles have to swerve off the road on their side, and eventuallly all ways are blocked, and everything in both directions comes to a complete standstill.

A Filipino friend once told me, "We like to regard traffic rules as suggestions." When the "suggestion" does not suit the driver, the tendency is simply to ignore it. Going through lights after they have turned red; crossing "stop" lines; going the wrong way down a one-way street; changing lanes to gain a tiny distance in heavy traffic; sounding the horn every few minutes for no apparent reason: these are some of the bad road habits of the Filipinos.

Road Rage

The first time I allowed my driver to use our new four-wheel-drive car, he only had to go five minutes down the road. However, on the way back he cut in front of another car and turned right in front of it. Contact was made. The mud-flap on our car was torn and the front bumper of the other car came off. The other driver jumped out, holding a steel pipe. My driver sat in the car while he walked around it, hitting it with the pipe! Later, at the police station, the other driver said to me, "Your driver drove in such an arrogant way. If my daughter had been in the car, and if I had had a gun, I would have shot him."

We learned from this incident that if you put an expensive new car in the hands of your driver he feels he is the most important person on the road; and that Filipinos often carry steel pipes, baseball bats, and even guns with them, and are prepared to use them, particularly to defend their families.

The normally easygoing, polite Filipino seems to change personality behind the wheel of a car. He will show no consideration toward others, be they drivers or pedestrians. For example, if you attempt to enter a main road from a side street, no one will give way to you; you will have to push in, forcing someone to slow down. Driving is a stressful experience throughout the country, and the traffic jams in and around Manila make it worse. Many foreigners prefer not to drive. For those on foot, pedestrian crossings are hardly a safer place to cross a road than anywhere else.

Jeepneys

The jeepney is a unique form of public transportation that is distinctively Filipino. Its design is based on the surplus U.S. army jeeps that were much in evidence after World War II.

Beside the driver sit his friends or preferred passengers, and everybody else squeezes on to the two rows of benches behind. The vehicle opens at the back to enable passengers to get in and out.

Each jeepney has its route painted on the side, and the driver must follow that route. He is paid by his company according to the number of passengers he carries per day, so will stop

anywhere to pick people up, oblivious to the motorists who are forced to wait behind him with his exhaust fumes in their faces. Fares are very cheap—under P5 (about 10 cents) for the first four kilometers. When riding in a jeepney, knock on the roof to indicate that you want to stop.

Jeepneys are brightly painted and decorated with names and slogans. Small figures of horses or wild animals are placed on the hood to suggest power, which the driver will use to the full, and pennants flutter from aerials. Appearance is all-important: money is spent on accessories while the tires, particularly the spare, may have little or no tread. Once again, the fatalism of *Bahala Na* is in evidence. There may also be a Christian message, such as "God bless you!" on the windshield, a rosary hanging on the mirror inside, and a statue of the Virgin Mary on the dashboard. The religious blends with the superstitious, since these symbols are intended to guarantee a safe journey whatever the driving habits of the driver.

Buses

Buses are operated by franchises or private owners and are generally not well maintained. They emit noxious gases and frequently break down, exacerbating the traffic jams. The government has now introduced testing of exhaust emissions, and on certain roads, particularly EDSA, the main thoroughfare in Manila, buses that emit black smoke will be called over for a test. If they fail the test, a fine is due within forty-eight hours. However, the fines are so small that most owners pay immediately and put the vehicle back on the road without carrying out any repairs. Low maintenance enables owners to charge low fares. On the other hand, it also maximizes profits, and this is the primary reason for owners being unwilling to reduce gas emissions. The newer, air-conditioned buses are generally better maintained, and the fares are a little higher.

Long-distance buses are a popular means of transport for Filipinos traveling to visit their families in the provinces. These often travel overnight from Manila to other parts of the island of Luzon, and are more reliable than those in Manila itself.

Taxis

When you arrive at Ninoy Aquino International Airport, always take an airport or hotel car, or a taxi that is part of a franchise. As in most cities, there are dishonest drivers who will exploit unsuspecting visitors. Efforts to clear the airport of such drivers have been successful, but it is still important to be careful.

Unscrupulous taxi drivers do exist in town, and the safest advice there is to take a taxi from a hotel, where the registration number will be logged. When you start the journey, make sure the driver turns on the meter; if he tries to negotiate a fare, he wants to cheat you.

Most taxi drivers are totally honest, however,

and will even, if they can, return an item left in the taxi by a passenger. Many speak some English, and communication is not a great problem, although it may be useful to have the address of your destination written down. The taxis in Manila are cheap and plentiful—although when it rains they all seem to be occupied! They are generally air-conditioned, and have seatbelts. The drivers expect a tip, especially if you are a foreigner; but this is not obligatory.

RAIL

The Light Rail Transit (LRT) and the Metro Rail Transit (MRT) provide a fast and comfortable journey. The LRT has been in operation for about twenty years, and the MRT is relatively new, with extensions still under construction. The MRT, which runs along EDSA, brings commuters into and out of the Central Business District of Makati. The trains are air-conditioned, and offer an excellent alternative to those who wish to avoid traffic jams. However, your destination needs to be within walking distance of the MRT station.

FERRIES AND BOATS

With the Philippines being made up of so many islands, ferries have traditionally provided an efficient and cheap means of transportation between the islands, particularly Manila, the Visayas, and Mindanao. Following a number of disasters, primarily due to overloading of passengers and cargo, the government has introduced strict regulations. Long-distance ferries now have better facilities, with different classes of accommodation available. Tickets are available in the harbor area, in some shopping malls, and at some travel agents.

If you travel a short distance between islands, you will probably travel by *banca*, the Filipino outrigger with an outboard or inboard motor. These are often unstable when the sea is rough, and it is essential to establish with the crew in advance what weather conditions are expected.

AIR

There are flights to destinations throughout the country. Although concerns are often expressed about the flightworthiness of some aircraft, on the whole the safety record within the country has been good. During the Filipino summer and at Christmas flights are heavily booked and one needs to apply well in advance.

PLACES TO VISIT IN AND AROUND MANILA

As a city of around eleven million people, and covering an area of nearly 270 square miles (approx. 700 sq. km.), Manila—often referred to as Metro Manila—is the seat of government, the financial center, and the economic hub of the country. Manila's long history results from its situation as a natural port in a huge bay, and many of the sights have historical significance. These include Intramuros, Fort Santiago, Malacanang Palace (with the three thousand pairs of shoes belonging to Imelda Marcos!), Ermita, Malate, Makati, Fort Bonifacio, and Corregidor.

PLACES TO VISIT AWAY FROM MANILA

The Philippines is a beautiful country, with rugged mountain ranges, sandy beaches, and clear blue seas. To enjoy all these, and to meet the friendly Filipinos away from urban Manila, try to visit as many of the following as possible: Tagaytay, Lake Taal, and Taal volcano; Laguna and Pagsanjan; Subic/Olongapo and Clark/Angeles; Baguio and Banaue; Cebu, Mactan, and Bohol; Boracay; Palawan; and Mindanao. There is a range of accommodation, from luxury hotels to inexpensive tourist inns and camp sites. Boracay also offers bamboo huts with palm-frond roofs.

HEALTH
Cleanliness

The Filipinos take great pride in their appearance. Given that many live in poor areas with no running water, it is amazing that they always leave home looking immaculate.

Office workers would never wear the same outfit on consecutive days. And probably in no other country in the world would all office workers bring toothbrush and toothpaste to work as a matter of course (after lunch, without fail, they all brush their teeth). Schoolchildren's shirts and blouses are always clean and white—at least at the beginning of the day! And every Sunday household helpers leave their working clothes at home and turn out beautifully dressed and groomed for their day off.

On the other hand, washing one's hands after going to the toilet is not thought important. This poses difficulties for restaurant managers who try to impose good standards of hygiene.

One complaint that Filipinos have about foreigners is that they smell! Western visitors may not realize that a much more powerful deodorant is needed in the tropics. If you are alone in a lift, the doors open on the next floor, and nobody gets in, it is not because you are the boss. It's probably because of your smell—and for cultural reasons you won't be told the truth.

> **And Now Wash Your Hands!**
> It is essential that everybody in your household washes their hands before touching food. The importance of this cannot be overemphasized. Our ten-year-old son caught typhoid from our cook, who turned out to be a carrier.

Despite attempts to clean up the city of Manila, progress is slow. People continue to throw litter everywhere. Last year, the shortage of landfill sites led to piles of garbage left at the sides of roads, and in some areas people started burning the garbage, creating noxious fumes.

One commonly sees men urinating against a wall or the wheel of a bus or jeepney. Some people joke that the bad smell around newly constructed buildings comes from mixing cement with urine. Although portable toilets are becoming more common at large events and on building sites, the fact remains that there are no constructed public toilets beside the road, and travel time for Filipinos is considerable, given the bad traffic.

In the dirt, pollution, and hot, humid weather, it is not surprising that rodents abound, mosquitoes breed, and various diseases and ailments are prevalent.

Water

Do not drink tap water. If you are a resident, you can have drinking water delivered to your home in gallon bottles. Some companies offer a water dispenser free with a minimum weekly order. If you 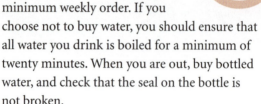 choose not to buy water, you should ensure that all water you drink is boiled for a minimum of twenty minutes. When you are out, buy bottled water, and check that the seal on the bottle is not broken.

In the hot weather, people enjoy cold drinks with ice. This is usually safe in hotels and good restaurants. However, you will see vans delivering huge blocks of ice that melt and drip on the road. A couple of men drag the ice along the ground to the back of a restaurant. There it is cut into smaller blocks and kept in freezers. When ice is required for a drink, a piece is chiseled off. You can play it safe by asking for "no ice" in your drink, especially if traveling out of town.

Take Care of Yourself

Visitors may suffer from stomach upsets and diarrhea. This may just be a reaction to a change in diet or water, and is usually mild compared with the infamous "Delhi Belly." Provided you are careful what and where you eat (avoid roadside stalls, for example), you should not suffer too much. (Nevertheless, a frequent excuse from Filipino staff for being absent from work is "LBM," or loose bowel movement.)

Dehydration may result from diarrhea, exposure to excessive heat, or strenuous exercise. It is essential to drink plenty of fluids and to wear clothing that will protect you from the sun. At the beach, limit the time you spend in the sun, put on high-factor sunscreen, and wear sunglasses. Children should wear specially made sun-protective swimwear.

A young European may wear a baseball cap as a fashion accessory, but in the Philippines such headwear is a necessity. Construction site workers and others who spend the day in the sun wrap towels around their heads and necks. The baseball caps keep them in place.

The number of cases of asthma continues to rise as pollution worsens. At certain times of the day a cloud of pollution can be seen over Manila. The solution is to escape to the hills or to the beach as often as possible. Some people use air cleaners, and the wealthy keep air-conditioning on throughout the day in the home, in an effort to reduce the amount of airborne substances and dust. Otherwise, keep windows closed as much as possible, and use fans.

Fever

While malaria has been virtually eradicated from urban areas, another mosquito-transmitted disease, which can be fatal, is dengue fever. The *Aedes aegypti* mosquito, which can be identified by stripes on its legs, bites during the day. The incubation period is five to eight days. Symptoms are fever, pains in the head, back, eyes, and joints, and sometimes a rash on arms and legs. There is no specific drug for dengue fever. Treatment consists of bed rest, increased fluid intake, and acetaminophen (Tylenol or Paracetamol). Do not take aspirin, which may aggravate hemorrhagic bleeding. A blood test can confirm if the patient has dengue fever. There is no preventive vaccine.

"H" fever is distinguished from classic dengue fever by hemorrhagic bleeding from the nose, through the skin, or internally. Symptoms appear between the second and fifth days of classic dengue fever, and include cold, clammy extremities, rapid but weak pulse, abdominal pain, mental confusion, and/or stupor. Anyone suffering from the classic form of dengue fever should watch out for these symptoms and seek immediate medical advice.

Hospitals are short of blood for transfusions, and if your blood type is uncommon they may not have a match. Ask the expatriate community and embassies about their blood registers.

> ### *Beware the Swimming Pool!*
> Unoccupied homes with swimming pools are dangerous. If a pool is not properly maintained by replenishing the chemicals, the water stagnates, and will become a likely breeding ground for the dengue-carrying mosquito.

Hepatitis

This is a common disease in the Philippines, and vaccinations against Hepatitis A and B are recommended.

Tuberculosis

TB is prevalent throughout Asia. Immunization (via the BCG vaccination) is essential, particularly for children, before your visit.

Household helpers and drivers often have TB, and must be screened before they come to work for you and then regularly (for example, annually) while they remain with you.

Typhoid Fever

Typhoid fever is easily passed through dirty water and poor hygiene practices, such as preparing food with unclean hands. It is contracted when food, water, or milk is contaminated with feces containing the typhoid bacteria. Everyone should always wash their hands before touching and eating food, and efforts must be made to keep flies away. Children must understand that only safe bottled or boiled drinking water may be consumed. Since typhoid is fairly common, the typhoid vaccination is recommended for added protection.

A preemployment medical examination of all your domestic staff, including a stool sample, is imperative, and they must be trained to pay special attention to cleanliness.

AIDS

Since the Filipinos are generally socially conservative, AIDS has not become a serious problem in the Philippines. Fewer than 2,000 cases of HIV/AIDS have been reported since 1984. However, in September 2003, when the Health Secretary reported a significant increase in sexually transmitted infections, he warned that this might indicate an increase in the number of AIDS cases in the future. Visitors should take nothing for granted.

MEDICAL CARE

Filipinos believe in both Western and alternative medicine. Many doctors have received training in the United States, and the medical and nursing schools are based on the U.S. system. Thus, they are generally very competent. The problem is the shortage of medical personnel and hospital beds. The U.S.A. and the U.K. are currently employing thousands of Filipino nurses. The number of nurses who apply to go overseas and earn much more money exceeds the demand, and Western employers naturally choose the best. It is even reported that some doctors are retraining as nurses so that they can go overseas. This clearly has a serious effect on medical care in the Philippines.

The country has a social security system, including medicare, with wide coverage of the regularly employed urban workers. However, as a developing country, the government has limited resources available for health care. Thus, there is a great disparity between private and public hospitals, with the latter generally being understaffed and ill equipped. The poor receive free medical care, but have to pay for their medicine; this often causes great anxiety.

The strain on the medical system, even in private hospitals, is exacerbated by the readiness with which Filipinos call on it for the slightest ailment. A child with a fever is taken to the doctor and may be treated with antibiotics. A child suffering from dehydration stays in the hospital and an IV drip is inserted.

If you as a foreigner fall ill or have an accident when you are traveling in the provinces, you should seek immediate treatment there, but try to get to a hospital in the main city, preferably Manila or Cebu, as soon as possible. Hospitals and doctors' clinics are always crowded, because Filipinos accompany their family members to medical appointments. Many doctors do not accept appointments, and see patients on a first-come-first-served basis. Hospital in-patients who pay for a private room may have their family there overnight. The very wealthy take suites, and the patient brings a maid and/or a private nurse to provide additional care. Hence nurses at private hospitals are quite surprised that foreigners "stay alone" in the hospital, and that they are expected to look after the patient. It is also common practice (as in most Asian cultures) that the patient does not eat the hospital food. It is part of caring for the sick that home-cooked food is brought to the patient three times a day.

Efforts are made to ensure that hospitals are kept clean, but there are concerns about the possibility of infection following operations.

Local Filipinos will sometimes refer to Makati Medical Center, the largest private hospital in Manila, as Makati Dead! Another concern is that some doctors are particularly eager to diagnose a serious medical problem, requiring extensive treatment, when they learn that the patient is covered by medical insurance.

Buying Medicine

Don't be surprised, when purchasing tablets at the pharmacy, if you are asked, "How many pieces?" Many Filipinos are paid daily for their work, and cannot afford the full course of medicine at once, so tablets are often sold individually. Ask for the instructions that come with the packaging.

When one's household helper or driver is diagnosed with a disease, particularly tuberculosis, expatriates are advised not to give the sick person money for the medication, but to buy it themselves. This means the money will not be spent on other things!

Alternative Medicine

While urban Filipinos have largely adopted Western medicine, those originally from rural areas still believe in home remedies and traditional healing techniques. The traditional approach to healing often assumes that illness is caused by a breach of taboos set by supernatural forces. (An expatriate with a back problem called in a masseur, who told him that it would not be easy to solve the problem because the gnomes in the garden were angry.) Generally, however, it is not uncommon for Western and folk medicine to be conducted side by side.

Chinese oils and ointments are much used for soothing muscles, and other Chinese medicines are taken to relieve headaches and sore throats. Reflexology is popular, and carried out by a good practitioner the benefits can be significant.

The Philippines is considered to be a world center for faith healing, where religious and folk practices are intermingled. Folk healers, who have always been held in high esteem in their village community, adopted a holistic approach to healing, so that the physical, emotional, and spiritual needs are met concurrently. With the spread of Christianity, the folk healers may often be considered faith healers, since they have a profound Christian faith and adopt Church practices. Holy water may be sprinkled on the patient, the sign of the cross made on the forehead with the fingers dipped in oil, and hands laid on the afflicted part of the body. Then prayers will be said, and there may be chanting.

Faith or folk healers may be regarded as allies

whose work can complement modern health practices. The doctor diagnoses the condition and provides a cure to the extent possible under Western medicine, but the faith healer can provide the psychological, emotional, and spiritual well-being necessary to the healing process. When the patient believes he is cured, he will return to the doctor for confirmation.

SAFETY

The media have made much of crime in the Philippines, and many outsiders now think that it is a dangerous country to visit. But do not be put off. True, terrorism has not been eliminated, and foreigners do sometimes become victims of crime in Manila; but if you are aware of the dangers and take sensible precautions it is as safe as most big cities anywhere, though certain places are no-go areas. It is a matter of using common sense and keeping your wits about you. Take care of your valuables at all times, and don't walk along a dimly lit street at night, especially if you are wearing expensive jewelry.

Terrorism is a concern. There has been violence in Mindanao for decades, with the local Communists and the Muslim separatist groups fighting the Manila government. Indications of the presence of Al Qaeda increased the anxiety of the Americans, in particular, and U.S. troops have been permitted to play an advisory role and train the Filipino military in Mindanao.

The Abu Sayyaf Group (ASG), is funded through bombings, assassinations, kidnappings, and extortion, and its successful raid on Dos Palmas, an island off Palawan, has had a bad effect on tourism in the area. Such groups are not driven by ideology, but may rather be regarded as bandits seeking to make a fast buck. The sooner they are destroyed, the better it will be for tourism.

Tricksters

Most criminal activities against foreigners, however, tend to involve confidence tricks or stealing. Some Filipinos use their natural creativity and charm for their own ends, and consider that if they can outwit a foreigner they deserve their reward. Foreigners are easily duped if they are not aware of some common strategies. The main points to remember are: never get into a car with strangers or go off with them, however friendly they may appear; never accept food or drink from them, however innocent it may seem; never turn your back on your drink; and never leave your valuables unattended. Drinks and food can be drugged, and the innocent tourist swiftly robbed.

A certain trick is sometimes played on foreigners visiting tourist sites. A smiling man hands you his camera, and politely asks you to take a photograph of him. You do so, and return the camera, but he stays with you and begins a long, friendly conversation. Eventually he invites you to his house, where he provides you with food, drink, and entertainment. Then he demands that you pay him a large sum of money or suffer unpleasant consequences.

Beware, also, of the unknown telephone caller with an "introduction," such as, "We met at a party recently," or "I am a friend of someone you know." He is probably trying to elicit a name from you. If you say something like, "Did we meet at Juan Gutierrez' party?" or "Are you a friend of Rey Gonzalez?" he now has a name to use, and is on the way to gaining your confidence. He will soon tell you some story about your friend being in some trouble, or very busy, unable to get to the bank, and needing to borrow money that he (the caller) will come and collect from you.

The most successful telephone con man in the Philippines in recent years was in fact not a Filipino but an Australian, who managed to convince a large number of expatriates that he needed money for an emergency, giving an assurance that he would repay them. He was eventually caught and deported.

Daylight Robbery

As in any city in the world, there are incidents of "mugging," or robbery with violence, but as a visitor you would be more likely to fall victim to a pickpocket or a team of well-organized tricksters. They act quickly, so be on your guard at all times.

Some operate in expensive hotels in Manila. For example, at the checkout desk a businessman puts his briefcase down while he pays the bill. It takes only a few seconds for one person to distract him, another to snatch the briefcase containing his ticket, passport, and other valuables, and for a third to disappear outside with it.

Don't leave your briefcase, bag, or purse on the floor or hanging on the back of your chair while you are eating in a restaurant. Put them carefully where you can see them, out of reach of anyone else. In shopping malls, be careful if someone bumps into you. He or she may have an accomplice who is waiting to snatch your wallet or cell phone while your attention is diverted. Someone may crouch in front of you to tie up a shoelace as you approach an escalator. As you stop or hesitate, an accomplice removes your money from your backpack.

Credit Card Fraud

In many Asian countries, credit card cloning is on the increase. Credit cards posted by the banks do not always reach their intended recipients, but are intercepted and used. As a precaution against this, you should instruct your bank, in writing, not to mail you a credit card in an envelope that can be recognized.

If you use a credit card to pay for a meal in a restaurant, don't let it out of your sight. The details could be copied to make up an identical card, which could be widely used before you know what is happening.

CONCLUSION

Security concerns should certainly not prevent visitors from enjoying all that the country has to offer. However, it is wise to be always alert to the possibility of being the victim of a scam or a theft, and to take sensible precautions, as one would do anywhere in the world.

chapter **seven**

BUSINESS BRIEFING

A blend of Western and Eastern beliefs, values, and lifestyle has resulted in an approach to business that is unique to the Philippines. On the surface, so much is familiar that the newly arrived foreigner might be led to think that Western business practices predominate. English is the language of business; many Filipino senior executives have attended universities in the United States; and the key element of the Constitution is democracy. However, any assumption that business can be conducted in the same way as in the United States or Europe will inevitably result in misunderstandings and disappointments that are likely to be detrimental to your objectives.

OFFICE ETIQUETTE AND PROTOCOL

It is important for foreign executives to create the right impression on their Filipino colleagues and subordinates. In order to achieve this, it is necessary for them to understand various aspects of office etiquette and protocol.

Attire

Despite comparatively low salaries, managers and office staff dress smartly and are well groomed. Long hair for men, even tied back, is rare, and is unacceptable in a business environment. Managers wear either Western-style suits or the *barong Tagalog,* a lightweight shirt with long or short sleeves, which is worn over an undershirt. The *barong* can be intricately embroidered for formal occasions, in lieu of a tuxedo, or plain for daily office wear; there are tailors in every shopping mall who will make one for you. It is ideal for a warm climate, and is never worn with a jacket. Unless the air-conditioning is particularly strong, the jacket of a Western suit is worn only at a formal meeting.

Female managers may wear a suit, preferably with a skirt rather than pants, or a well-cut dress. Most Filipinas dress modestly, with no miniskirts or plunging necklines; but there are always exceptions!

In some companies, employees are not required to dress so smartly on Fridays, when many employees (not the managers) wear jeans.

Greetings

Every day, as you arrive at the office, remember to greet each member of your staff with a cheerful

"Good morning" and a smile. Whenever you visit your boss, stop to exchange a few words with his or her secretary. Treating people as individuals and establishing a rapport pays dividends in the long run—for example, the secretary will ensure that your boss gets that urgent message from you before she goes home.

Forms of Address

Filipinos place importance on status and seniority. It is therefore unusual for subordinates to call or refer to managers by their first names. If a foreigner asks his secretary to use his first name, it may be regarded as a desire for equality, which, in that setting, is alien to traditional Filipino culture. The secretary may become too independent, and consult the boss less frequently, until the boss feels he has to draw her attention to the matter. The misunderstanding may have long-term effects on their relationship. The boss should be addressed as "Sir" or "Ma'am," or formally, using "Mr.," "Mrs.," or "Miss," and the surname.

Even among the office staff there are hierarchies based on age as well as seniority: the supervisor may be called "Ma'am" or "Sir" before their first name, as in "Sir Chito." In addition, the oldest and most respected female employee in a particular office may be referred to as "*Manang*" (older woman) or "*Tita*" (Auntie) before her first name, as in "*Tita* Marge." Similarly, for the men, the address will be "*Manong*" (older man), which may be abbreviated to "*Man*," as in "*Man* Lito."

Professionals are addressed by their title. For example, you will hear, "It's a pleasure to meet you, Attorney Gonzales." Don't be surprised if you are introduced to Engineer Ramos and Architect Reyes. And all politicians and officials, current and past, keep their titles forever, for example, Mayor Bunye, or Justice Lopez.

Timekeeping

Punctuality is not as important to the Filipinos as it is to Westerners. There are many excuses for being late to work, the main one for those in Metro Manila being the traffic. There is often justification for this, such as when there is localized flooding or a road accident, when traffic comes to a standstill.

On a personal level, humor can be more effective than confrontation or direct criticism. When one of your staff arrives late to work for the second time that week, it will not help to frown and say, "Why are you late again?" It would be better to joke, "Gina, you really must stop having such late nights out with all your boyfriends!" In teasing her, you will have conveyed the message that her tardiness has been observed and is not acceptable.

However, for the Filipinos, it is customary to be late for meetings, just as it is for social gatherings. The punctual foreigner may be frustrated at having to wait for the Filipinos to arrive, and so, at the time that the meeting schedule is set, there is no harm in saying, with a smile, "Is that American or Filipino time?" The smile will indicate that you are not being critical but want to ensure you do not have to wait around for the others. Changes are taking place, and business meetings do start more promptly than in the past, but the foreigner must realize that the late arrival of other participants is in no way intended as a personal slight. On the other hand, foreigners are expected to be punctual!

Teamwork

In any country, teamwork is a major ingredient of success, but this is even more true in the Philippines. When Filipino employees working together on a project bond as a group, they will go out of their way to help each other in order to maximize productivity and achieve success. On the other hand, if there is any conflict between them they find it difficult to put aside personal differences and get on with the task at hand. One has caused another to lose face, a petty dispute has got out of hand, or resentment has resulted from one person trying to assert authority over another. The manager needs to be aware of such conflicts to select a harmonious team for a particular project, even though it may mean omitting a potential contributor who does not get along with the others. The importance of *pakikisama* must not be underestimated.

Birthdays

Birthday celebrations are a feature of office life. The person whose birthday it is brings or orders in some snacks and cakes. However heavy the workload, everything comes to a halt, and everyone in the team, including the boss, joins in the party. If the boss were absent without a good reason, he or she would be regarded as aloof or arrogant. To take time out of a busy day for socializing is not to waste it. In fact not to do so might be counterproductive in the long term.

MANAGEMENT STYLE

The Filipinos place value on status, and have a genuine respect for those in authority. As a result, they are generally compliant. Believing that the boss is probably better qualified and has wider work experience, they readily accept his or her leadership.

Filipino managers tend to adopt a paternalistic style. Thus, while they require their staff to work hard, carry out their instructions, and never rock the boat, they also have due concern for their welfare. The manager spends time establishing a relationship with his or her staff members, and learning about their individual circumstances. It is important also to gain the support and trust of a Filipino supervisor who can act as a go-between.

In the event of a personal emergency, such as a sick child, the manager may be a little flexible regarding working hours. An employee who tried to take advantage of the manager, or conceal the truth, would be breaching this trust. The manager would be offended and would discipline the employee. If a female staff member were involved the likely outcome would be tears, since Filipinas are not afraid to show emotion.

Having heard tales of foreigners being tricked, a foreign manager may sometimes wonder whether such a personal emergency is genuine, and this is where a go-between is invaluable.

If a manager has to reprimand a staff member, this must be done behind closed doors. Verbal abuse is not acceptable in Filipino culture, and a public dressing-down would bring shame on the individual concerned. Even in private, avoid showing anger toward the employee. Take the time and trouble to find out what his or her problems are, and give guidance for future behavior.

The main strength of the Filipinos lies in their ability to follow clear instructions. It is therefore worth the manager's while to ensure that each staff member knows exactly what is required of him or her. The main weakness relates to written reports: the written English of many Filipinos does not match the quality of their spoken English; there is also generally a lack of in-depth analysis, a result of the education system, which requires regurgitation of facts, as well as the cultural inclination to follow rather than question. Thus, even though your staff may have college degrees, their strengths and weaknesses will be different from those of Western graduates.

Another weakness concerns quality control. Completion of a task is often regarded as being the primary objective, even if the quality does not match expectations. Preventive maintenance work is not given due importance—why spend money when the machine is working perfectly well?

It is not suggested that foreigners should automatically adopt the management style of Filipino managers. It is expected that the management style of a foreigner will be different. Similarly, you cannot expect Filipinos to work as Westerners do. But you should understand the differences, learn from the Filipinos, and encourage them to learn from you too.

WEEVILS IN THE MILK POWDER

The foreign manager of a factory making dried milk powder for babies left for his summer vacation. After a week, he received an alarming telephone call. Weevils had been found in the milk powder, and manufacturing had to stop immediately until the bugs were eradicated.

He returned immediately to Manila and questioned his Filipino supervisor, who confirmed that there were arrangements in place for a company to spray the factory every month to stop bugs from breeding. But when they came last month, the supervisor had been very busy, and he told them to come back another day. After a week he realized that they hadn't returned, but as it was then only three weeks until the next spraying, and there appeared to be no problem with bugs, he didn't contact them. It took several weeks to get rid of the weevils, and this cost the company a huge sum of money.

Filipino management style would give less independence to the supervisor. The foreign manager assumed the supervisor was doing his job properly, and had not checked up on him for some time. As a result, without the monitoring from above, the supervisor had become lax.

The foreigner will be expected to adjust to certain facets of Filipino life, such as birthdays or the death of a family member. Death is a truly sad event. Colleagues of the bereaved attend the wake of a parent, and an envelope may be passed around the office for a contribution toward the cost of the wake and funeral, or for flowers. You should make a contribution and attend the wake, particularly if it is the spouse of one of your staff who has died. As you understand and apply Filipino cultural values and practices, so your staff will be more willing to take on your methods of increasing efficiency and productivity.

Expressing and Managing Disagreement

Filipinos strive for smooth personal relationships, and therefore avoid direct confrontation or criticism. When they disagree with one of the manager's work objectives, or fail to see the benefit of undertaking a particular task, they keep quiet, but take no action to complete the job. Requests for an update on progress are met with excuses for delays and assurances that the work will be completed as soon as possible. The Filipino manager will by this time have realized that there is a problem that needs to be discussed.

The foreign manager must understand that silence is not necessarily a sign of agreement.

Even a nod and a "Yes, Sir" may only be an acknowledgment that the instructions have been heard, for they may not have been fully understood, let alone agreed to. Admitting to not understanding would be too embarrassing, and would be contrary to the values of *hiya* and *amor propio*. Open disagreement with the manager would not be expressed in front of outsiders. Face-to-face, disagreement or constructive criticism would be prefixed with a softener, such as, "Your suggestion is very interesting, but don't you think . . . ," or "Please correct me if I am wrong, but . . ."

If you, as manager, have doubts about the meaning of a response, you should watch to ensure that work proceeds promptly and in accordance with your instructions. However, this takes valuable time, and might cause the working relationship to deteriorate. Therefore it is extremely useful to establish a good rapport with the senior Filipino employee in your department. As supervisor, he or she is in a position to provide you with honest feedback and to act as a go-between, and should be encouraged to do so. He or she may also be used in the same way by staff wishing to express a concern to you. Keep a cool head, use the supervisor to convey your message, and the result is likely to be positive.

SPEECHES AND PRESENTATIONS

Filipinos have a great sense of humor, and love to be entertained. The spontaneous and witty speaker will quickly become a favorite. Presidential candidates who were formerly actors gain votes through popularity. Reason and ideology win fewer votes than entertainment or, of course, regional or family allegiances.

At a training seminar, it is necessary to hold the attention of the participants, and humor is a useful tool for this purpose. However, evaluation of a workshop facilitator may be based more on entertainment value than on the achievement of objectives and their relevance to the work of the participants.

When you are making a presentation, it is a good idea to tell an amusing story to establish a rapport with the audience. (Be careful: as a foreigner, avoid criticism of the Philippines or of any individuals. Despite their sense of humor, they would not be amused if the story were to cause any loss of face.) Once you have the audience's attention and a positive attitude, your message will be a great deal more effective.

The situation is a little different when you are making a presentation to executives, who require less entertainment and more factual information. Nevertheless, humor makes the speaker seem less austere

THE MOTIVATIONAL ADDRESS

A foreign head of department decided it was time to deliver a motivational address to his 150 staff members. He would congratulate them on their efforts, encourage them to work harder, and outline his plans for the coming year. He hoped they would give him feedback on their concerns, and perhaps some useful suggestions.

He knew that some of them would have to remain at their desks to deal with enquiries, so he was pleased that 90 percent were present when he began his talk. He noticed a few chins fall on to chests and some eyes glaze over, but the rest seemed attentive and so he continued for about thirty minutes, then asked for comments or questions. One person stood and asked politely, "Sir, when will we be told the amount of our annual salary increase?"

He was surprised at the question because salaries were not his responsibility. However, he gave a brief answer and asked for more questions. There were none. He asked, "Do you understand the plans for the coming year?" Everyone nodded. "Do you believe we can accomplish these objectives?" Everyone nodded. He thought he had their support.

Over the next year, he experienced a great deal of frustration as people dragged their feet. He came to realize that they hadn't been convinced, and were only reluctantly carrying out his instructions. He had to learn some lessons:

- Filipinos follow instructions, so a high turnout is to be expected.
- Without any humorous anecdotes, the attention of the listeners is soon lost.
- Nodding is not to be taken as agreement, nor is a "Yes." The staff would not question the boss or express doubts about his plans.
- The immediate concern of Filipinos is their salary, for the good of their family.
- Unless the Filipinos fully appreciate the benefits of a planned course of action, they drag their feet, giving excuses for delays.
  Only when asked point-blank do they finally question the value of what they have been asked to do.
- It is often helpful to have a senior Filipino member of staff who can be relied upon to give you honest feedback.

and more approachable. Since Filipinos want to establish good interpersonal relations with business partners, it still has a valuable role to play. But avoid sensitive topics such as politics, corruption, sex, and religion.

MEETINGS AND NEGOTIATIONS

It is very unlikely that you will be able to arrange a meeting with a senior Filipino executive unless you work for an international organization or a multinational company; or know someone who is in a position of influence to set up the meeting on your behalf. In other words, you are worth meeting only if you have the right status in a respected company, or if you are introduced by a mutual friend or business contact.

Many multinational companies retain the services of a retired politician or diplomat who can arrange meetings at the highest level and who can intercede on their behalf. The key to success in business is who you know, for this gives you the opportunity to explain what you know.

At the introductory meeting, time will be spent getting acquainted. First, be sure to address the executive formally, using his title, and then offer your business card. This will be kept for future reference, should the initial meeting proceed smoothly. A small gift with your company logo may also be given as a token of appreciation. Never rush into any business discussion: the first meeting is likely to be purely social.

Subsequently, a lunch can be arranged at which business issues of mutual interest can be raised after general conversation that further develops the relationship. However, the business discussion is unlikely to go very far. Progress may appear to be slow, with a round of golf being the occasion for the next meeting, but if the Filipino executive observes that the foreigner has integrity, sincerity, and intelligence, discussions can then proceed more quickly.

The foreigner should always respect the Filipino style of doing business and not display any signs of impatience, such as looking at his watch or using an irritated tone of voice. As the relationship develops, the foreigner may be invited to dinner at a restaurant, or even at home, as a sign of true acceptance. *Pakikisama* is the guiding force in the business relationship, and this takes time to develop.

For business meetings, especially those involving foreigners, an effort will be made to keep to the schedule. In the presence of a foreigner, English will be spoken throughout; otherwise the discussion would be a mixture of English and Filipino.

When a foreigner participates in negotiations

involving a number of personnel from his or her company and their counterparts, he or she must initially observe how discussions progress. Is it evident that the most senior person of the other company is authorized to make a decision, or will the matter have to be referred to a yet more senior executive? It is expected that most participants will chip in with their comments as details are discussed, and this can obviously prolong the meeting. It may seem as though little progress is being made on major issues.

Remember not to push too hard for an immediate resolution of an issue, and not to raise your voice. This would create the impression that you think you are always right as well as being insensitive to the nonconfrontational approach of Filipinos. You would be branded as arrogant, and business relationships would be adversely affected. Be patient and courteous.

If the discussion goes smoothly, matters will be forwarded to the next level of seniority. Legal documents will be prepared, spelling out the details of the contract. This stage progresses more swiftly. However, project implementation always takes longer than expected. Contractors blame subcontractors, and everyone blames the government for causing delays due to its bureaucratic procedures, as well as the weather and the traffic!

Doing Favors

The value of *utang na loob* (reciprocation of a favor) is prevalent in Filipino business. If A helps B out of a difficult situation, he expects B to assist him when he is in a position to do so. So B should take care before asking a favor: he doesn't know what he will be asked to do in return.

The Favor

When studying for an examination, I found that I needed four books available only in the U.S.A. If I ordered them it would be weeks before they arrived, and I would have little time left for study. I knew a Filipino who had taken the examination the previous year, and I asked him if I could borrow his books. He readily lent them to me.

Some time later he came to see me. He wanted to leave his job and join a multinational company. Since I knew someone in the company, would I put in a word on his behalf? In Filipino culture, I had no choice but to return the favor, regardless of whether I considered him to be competent.

BUREAUCRACY AND CORRUPTION

In the Philippines, bureaucracy is a major obstacle to getting things done quickly and smoothly.

Paperwork abounds, with a number of signatures required before final approval is granted, and this takes time.

Cut through bureaucracy the Filipino way, and make use of a broker. This is a go-between who has daily contact with the individuals dealing with the necessary paperwork. A broker can accelerate clearance procedures by paying the right amount of money to the right people. If a foreigner were to get involved personally, a much larger payment would be expected, and there would be no guarantee that everyone involved had received something.

Civil servants who assist your company through the efficient processing of papers expect a small gift at Christmas. You should make sure that no one who deserves a gift is left out!

Is this really corruption? In Filipino, it is called *lagay*, a small bribe, but euphemisms include "persuasive communication" and "facilitation fee." On a small scale this is generally accepted. At the clerical level, civil servants' salaries are so low that the workers need to supplement their income to support their families. The view of recipients of *lagay* is that family is more important than ethical considerations relating to the receipt of money from people who can afford it, in return for speeding up processing of documentation. On the other hand, this is a sliding scale. At higher levels in government service, graft can be more serious. Elections are often bloody, not only because of rivalries between families, but because of the kickback involved, even at the level of mayor.

The foreigner should be wary of getting involved in any corrupt practices. It is a minefield, which even Filipinos pass through at their peril. President Estrada proved to be too greedy, and action was taken to replace him. It is hoped that the tide has now turned in favor of more honest government.

WOMEN AT WORK

Philippine society is very different from most other Asian societies, in that women are given due professional respect and have excellent career opportunities. President Gloria Macapagal-Arroyo is the second female president of the Philippines, and her performance is as good as that of any of her male predecessors.

In the office, foreigners consider that Filipino women are generally more hardworking and more competent than men, and that they can be relied upon to complete the task assigned to them.

While Filipino men are trying to show how *macho* they are, sometimes even getting into fights, the women are distracted only by their family considerations. In fact, although men try to create the impression that it is they who wear the pants in the family, in most cases it is the woman who makes the decisions in the home and disciplines the children. Similarly, at work, women often take the lead, using their initiative and making creative suggestions.

> *Join In the Fun!*
> If you are in a position of leadership, have a song up your sleeve—you will be asked to sing at an office function. If you are invited to a party or event organized by one of your suppliers, be assured that you will be asked to participate in the evening's entertainment. The more important a client you are, the less chance you have of getting off the hook! You may also be asked to start off the dancing, pick the winning ticket for the raffle, or join in the karaoke!

GIFT GIVING

In general, the Filipinos place great value on imported gifts. If you want to please a local client, or signify that the relationship is important to you, give an expensive branded item. Within the office, the rule of thumb for a manager is consistency in value. A drop in the value of a birthday or Christmas gift from one year to the next may be perceived as indicating a change in the relationship. You must decide to whom you will give gifts in the office hierarchy without causing offense to others. Give birthday and Christmas presents at least to your secretary. When in doubt, on your own birthday bring in a large cake for everyone to share. And don't forget the *pasalubong,* the small gift that you bring back from your holiday for everyone directly under your supervision. You should give the same thing to everyone, with no variation except perhaps in the color.

CONCLUSION

The starting point for being a successful foreign businessman or woman in the Philippines is the willingness to put aside one's own cultural values and to leave behind the way one conducted business in one's own country. With an open mind, understand and try to appreciate the value of the Philippine approach to business. Then resolve to adopt it. This requires perception and patience, but it is worth it, because you will be working in a relaxed atmosphere and enjoying the company of your business partners.

chapter **eight**

COMMUNICATING

LANGUAGES

The Philippines is remarkable for its linguistic diversity. For geographic and demographic reasons, it is difficult even to estimate the number of languages and dialects spoken there. Some put the figure as high as 100 native languages and dialects plus a further 200 belonging to the Austronesian or Malayo-Polynesian family of languages. However, eight of the latter constitute the main languages that are spoken by large numbers of people.

LANGUAGE	AREA WHERE SPOKEN
Tagalog	Manila, South Central Luzon
Cebuano	Cebu and Northern Mindanao
Ilokano	Northern Luzon
Hiligaynon (Ilonggo)	Panay and Western Negros
Bikol	Southern Luzon
Waray Waray	Samar, Leyte
Kapampangan	Pampanga, Central Luzon
Pangalatok	Pangasinan, Central Luzon

In the 1930s an attempt was made to develop a national language based on the main languages used by Filipinos. In 1936, Tagalog was declared to be the basis of the national language, which was called Pilipino in 1959. However, non-Tagalog speakers objected to this, and some Congressmen made a point of using their own language when they spoke in Congress. In 1973, Pilipino was confirmed as the national language.

Given the strong regional allegiances in the Philippines, and the different languages used, when hiring household staff, it is always preferable that they come from the same province and speak the same language.

Filipino

Under the 1987 constitution, the national language was renamed Filipino, but English was also regarded as an official language. While Filipino is essentially Tagalog, words and phrases from other native languages, as well as from Spanish and English, have been incorporated. In today's world of technology, the number of words of English origin continues to increase.

As a foreigner in the Philippines, you can survive very easily without learning Filipino. However, if you can speak a few phrases, it will be greatly appreciated by Filipinos, who will believe that you are making an effort to understand not only the language but also the people. Also, in a shop where negotiation is expected, you are likely to get a better price if you speak a word or two of Filipino and the salesperson realizes that you are a local resident and not a tourist.

English

As a result of American influence, English is spoken widely throughout the country, especially among educated Filipinos. A taxi driver may speak limited English, but the office worker is expected to be reasonably proficient, although written English is of a much lower standard.

Filipinos are generally accustomed to American accents—from movies, and from the majority of English-speaking people they meet—and are less likely to understand a British or Australian accent. A sales assistant who does not understand you may, for cultural reasons, prefer to reply, "Out of stock," rather than ask you to repeat what you have said.

In the 1960s, the percentage of Filipinos speaking good English was higher than any other Asian country, but with the subsequent decline in English-language instruction in schools and the increased focus on English elsewhere in Southeast Asia, this is no longer the case. Today, the government acknowledges that English is necessary for international business, and is encouraging greater use of English in schools.

A few English words have been adopted by Filipinos to convey a unique meaning:

Blowout: Particularly on your birthday, you are expected to buy food so that your colleagues can celebrate with you. Providing food, or inviting them out for lunch or dinner, is a "blowout."

Brownout: A (usually daytime) power outage (power cut)—still a fairly common occurrence.

Maybe: This generally means "No." "Will you be able to finish that report by tomorrow?" If the response is "Maybe," or "I'll try," they mean they would like to help you, but it will not be possible. You are expected to understand that the report will *not* be ready by tomorrow. It is rare to be told a direct "No," because the Filipino does not want to displease you overtly.

Yes, meaning "No": On a purely linguistic level, "Yes" agrees with a negative statement: "You're not going to the party, are you?" "Yes." "You haven't got tickets to the concert, have you?" "Yes." In both cases, the "yes" signifies agreement, that is, "You're right, I'm not going to the party," "You're right, I haven't got tickets for the concert." In the office, the boss says, "You won't be late with that report, will you?" In British English, the expected response would be "No (I won't be late with the report)," whereas the Filipino response, with the same meaning, would be "Yes."

However, in general contexts "yes" also has broader cultural significance, which affects the true meaning of what Filipinos are saying. In order to avoid disappointment or confrontation, they will readily say "yes" when they do not actually agree. The reason for this may be to please you, or just to end the conversation! They may not be certain how to reply, and a verbal agreement is the more culturally acceptable response. To be sure that they really do mean "yes," look for a clue such as a nod, or enthusiasm in the tone of voice.

Spanish and Chinese

Over a hundred years since Spanish rule ended, some Filipinos of Spanish origin still speak Spanish at home. These tend to be families who have retained political or commercial influence. Gradually, as these families educate their children in the U.S.A., the use of Spanish is fading.

The Chinese have been migrating to the Philippines for about a thousand years and are a powerful merchant class. They generally marry within their own ethnic group, and still speak their dialect at home. The most widely spoken Chinese dialect is Hokkien.

Language in the Media

The widespread use of both English and Filipino is reflected in the publication of newspapers in both languages. On the whole, the quality papers are in English, and the rest are in Filipino. In addition, there is a Chinese newspaper.

Democracy has led to freedom of speech, and this is displayed very clearly in the press. One has to take political bias into account when trying to distinguish between fact and opinion. On the other hand, reading editorials is extremely enlightening, as they enable foreigners to gain a deeper understanding of Filipino culture and insights into the Filipino way of thinking.

TV has a variety of programs in English and Filipino. However, the "English" news can be frustrating for the foreigner. When reporters ask questions in English, the response may be in Filipino, or in English with a few Filipino words or phrases thrown in (this may be referred to as "Taglish"). Similarly, a program involving an interview with a well-known personality may end up as a mixture of English and Filipino. The switch between Filipino and English comes quite naturally, and occurs in everyday life at the office.

MEANS OF COMMUNICATION
Telephone
Within Metro Manila there is no charge for local telephone calls beyond the initial rental fee. Thus

Filipinos, who are naturally very sociable people, will talk for hours on the telephone.

Cell phones are used by nearly everybody today. The costs are considerably cheaper than in the U.S.A. and U.K. At the time of EDSA II, huge crowds assembled at the shrine on EDSA very quickly, because people were calling or texting their friends and encouraging them to join the rally. Filipinos claim that this was the first ever overthrow of a corrupt leader by text messaging! Similarly, rumors and jokes (for example, about politicians) spread rapidly by text messaging.

On the other hand, cell phones are easy spoil for thieves. Not only do pickpockets steal them, but on jeepneys and buses thieves will take out knives or guns and threaten the other passengers until they hand over their cell phones. It is best not to use a cell phone in a public place.

E-mail

E-mail is commonly used, and Internet cafés are extremely popular, especially among the young.

Postal Service

If you want to mail a letter, you must go to the post office. There are no mailboxes. The efficiency and reliability of the postal service has improved significantly over the past decade, but you are still advised to inform your bank in your home country not to send a credit card by mail. There are many cases of credit cards being detected, stolen, and used fraudulently by postal workers in the sorting office.

FACE TO FACE

Communication involves more than conveying a message using familiar words. Words have cultural significance, and the correct choice is important to ensure that no offense is caused; an appropriate tone expresses respect; and body language takes on additional importance in Philippine culture.

Forms of Address

The Filipinos are very respectful of authority and will give due respect to the status of the person they are addressing. This applies both in business relationships and in society as a whole. Thus, office staff normally address their manager as "Sir" or "Madam." The use of first names would imply a familiarity that, to the traditional Filipino, would undermine the status accorded to seniority. The expatriate wife who tells her domestic helper to call her by her first name creates a sense of awkwardness, and the helper may not be able to cope with this.

One may be used to addressing a medical doctor by his or her title, for example, "Dr. Brown." In the Philippines this also applies to other professionals, such as "Engineer Gutierrez," "Architect Lim," or "Attorney Santos." Until you have become friends with Filipinos, don't address them by their first names. Similarly, address those holding positions of civic importance according to their office, for example, "Mayor Binay," or "Mr. Mayor." The intention is to give people the self-esteem to which they are entitled. However, this practice goes beyond what might be expected. When a diner wants to attract the attention of a waiter, or a tennis player wants a ball boy to bring some water, he may call "Boss!" Through the giving of esteem, "Boss" softens the forthcoming instruction, so that it causes no offense.

Respect is also given to elders. Younger people will address older Filipinos by the word "*Po*." Sales assistants will also use it with older foreigners and say, "Thank you, *Po*." Thus, in this context, "*Po*" becomes a Filipinized "Sir."

On the other hand, if you are a Caucasian male foreigner, some street urchins may hail you with "Hi, Joe." This has developed from the fact that U.S. military personnel during the Second World War were known as GI Joe. You may find this irritating, but it is not intended to be offensive.

NONVERBAL LANGUAGE
Tone and Volume
The quickest way to spoil a relationship with employees or acquaintances is to shout at them—this causes loss of self-esteem, and at the same time shows that you are quarrelsome and arrogant. If you are also abusive in your words, this compounds the damage done by the tone and volume. If you must criticize someone, do so in private and without scolding. Be firm but polite.

Greetings
When you are introduced to a Filipino or Filipina, shake hands. If you know a lady well, a *beso-beso* (a kiss on each cheek, or just a touching of cheeks on each side) is acceptable. Recently, President Arroyo has been criticized for a public *beso-beso* with one of her cabinet ministers. However, among expatriates, this is the norm.

A typically Filipino greeting is the *mano po*, given, for example, by the respectful son of a colleague. He will bow to his elder, take his opposite hand, and respectfully place it to his own forehead. This ritual combines traditions from East and West. Particularly in Japan, bowing is a sign of respect, and elsewhere in the East it is accompanied by the kissing of the honored person's hand. The Western aspect comes from the clergy's demand for respect during the

Spanish occupation (which explains the word *mano*, Spanish for "hand"). Catholic priests and nuns kiss the Pope's ring to affirm their loyalty and recognize his authority over them. Similarly, the Spanish clergy required the Filipinos to kiss their hands.

Body Language
The Filipinos use various gestures or facial expressions to enhance communication or show respect. There are also certain actions that are considered rude. It is essential that you do not make wrong assumptions based on your own cultural background.

To be effective, communication must be two-way. Filipinos do communicate, but the foreigner must learn to understand the message that is being conveyed, since the words themselves are not necessarily the sole means of communication. Similarly, the foreigner must also control his or her tendency to speak bluntly, appreciate the need to avoid confrontation where possible, and ensure that the Filipino does not lose face.

Out of politeness, a Filipino does not like to walk between two people who are talking to each other. If it is necessary, he will do so, but he will lower his head, bend his knees, and extend one hand in front of him.

Filipinos are physically reserved with strangers,

but are completely different with friends. Girls often walk around hand in hand, and there is more physical contact between men than in the West, without any question that they are gay.

The raising and lowering of the eyebrows is a way of greeting someone. It is generally accompanied by a smile and conveys the message of a friendly "Hi." Avoid direct eye contact. Look briefly at someone, and then look away. It is considered rude to stare, and if you toss your head backward and make eye contact, this may be interpreted as a challenge.

Filipinos often indicate direction by pouting with their lips, or moving their eyes.

Smiles

Filipinos are often regarded as happy, smiling people—but the smile conveys many different feelings, apart from contentment. They smile when they are embarrassed, confused, apologetic, critical, or in disagreement. They want to avoid confrontation, and are concerned about "losing face." If a Filipino has made a mistake he will smile in the hope that you will not be angry. If a shop assistant is unable to help you, or cannot understand you, he will smile. When a waitress knocks over a glass of wine, she will smile. If you are the one who has made a mistake, a Filipino will smile and wait for you to recover your dignity. Do not think that he or she is laughing at you, or does not care about the mistake. This will not be the case.

> *DON'TS*
> - Don't snap your fingers to attract someone's attention.
> - Don't crook your finger or use a palm-upward motion to summon or beckon someone—bend your hand, palm down, at about chin height.

CONCLUSION

The Filipino people are warm, welcoming, sociable, industrious, and resilient. They are also highly sensitive to criticism and loss of face. In this book we have sought to equip you to build good relationships with the people you meet, and to find friends, gracious hospitality, and every reason to return again and again to these beautiful and fascinating islands.

Further Reading

History and Business

Agoncillo, Teodora A. *The Revolt of the Masses: The Story of Bonifacio and the Katipunan.*
Manila: University of the Philippines, 1996.

Canlas, Luzano P. *Philippines' 2 Millenium History.*
Maryland: Goodlife Publishing, 2000.

Gonzalez, Joaquin L., and Luis R. Calingo. *Culture Shock! Succeed in Business: Philippines.*
Singapore: Times Books International, 1998.

Karnow, Stanley. *In our Image: America's Empire.*
New York: Ballantine Books, 1990.

Nolan, James L., et al. *Philippines Business: Portable Encyclopedia for Doing Business with the Philippines (Country Business Guide).*
San Rafael, California: World Trade Press, 1996.

Roces, Alfredo and Grace. *Culture Shock! Philippines.*
Singapore: Times Books International, 1985.

Whitman, John W. Bataan. *Our Last Ditch: The Bataan Campaign, 1942.*
New York: Hippocrene Books, 1990.

Travel and Leisure

Alejandro, Reynaldo. *The Philippine Cookbook.*
New York: Coward McCann, 1982.

De Villa, Jill Gale. *Luzon by Car.*
Philippines: Devcon IP, 1985.

Dorai, Francis. *Insight Guide: Philippines.*
Insight Guides Philippines, 2000.

Grele, Dominique. *100 Resorts in the Philippines – Places with a Heart.*
Asiatype Incorporated, 2001.

Peplow, Evelyn. *The Philippines.*
Hong Kong: Odyssey Passport, 1997.

Rowthorn, Chris, et al. *Lonely Planet: Philippines.*
Melbourne/Oakland/London/Paris: Lonely Planet Publications, 2003.

The Action Asia Adventure Travel Guide to the Philippines.
Hong Kong: AAP Publishing, 1999.

Index

Abu Sayyaf Group 126
air travel 112
Al Qaeda 125
All Saints' Day 67–8
amor propio (sense of self, self-respect) 52, 54
area 10
Asia Pacific Economic Cooperation (APEC) 10
Association of Southeast Asian Nations (ASEAN) 10
asthma 117–18
Ati–Atihan festival 70–71
attitudes to foreigners 58–9
authority 55

Baguio 10, 14, 113
Bahala Na ("Leave it to God") 18, 56, 109
ballroom dancing 103
Banaue 113
banca (Filipino outrigger) 112
baptisms 84–5
Basilan 42
basketball 95–6, 97
birthdays 135
boats 112
body language 162–3
Bohol 113
Boracay 113
bowling 98
bureaucracy 147–8
buses 109–110
business entertaining 86–7

capital city 10
cars 106–8
Catholic Church 45, 60, 61, 66, 83, 101
Catholicism 8, 11, 23, 60, 61–2, 65, 68
Cebu 10, 21, 22, 71, 113, 122
chess 98–9
Chinese Filipinos 76
Christianity 23, 24, 25, 66, 72
Christmas 63–5

Clark/Angeles 113
cleanliness 114–15, 120
climate 10, 13–14
cockfighting 101
Communist Party of the Philippines (CPP) 36, 37
Corregidor 21
corruption 148–9
credit card fraud 128–9
criticism 136–7, 139, 161, 164
currency 11

dagal (self-respect based on what others think of one) 54
daily life and routines 77–9
Davao 10
dehydration 117, 122
dengue fever 118
Dinagyang festival 71
dress 131
drinks 87, 105, 116
drivers 92, 118

e-mail 158
earthquakes 17
Easter Sunday 66–7
economy 11, 44–5
EDSA II 41–4, 158
education 10, 25, 26, 30, 80, 137
Eid-al-Adzha 73
Eid-al-Fitr 72
El Shaddai 60–61
elderly, the 81–2
electricity 11, 53
employment overseas 45, 47–8
entertaining 86–9
environment 14–16

family 45, 46–50, 79–82
    celebrations 82–6
    compounds 75–6
ferries 111–12
fever 118–19
fiestas 68–72
food and drink 103–5
    table manners 105

forms of address 132–3, 159–60
funerals 85–6

gambling 100–101
geography 12–13
gifts 88–9, 144–5, 150–51
godparents 84–5
golf 96–7
Good Friday 65–6
government 11
greetings 131–2, 161–2

"H" fever 118–19
Halloween 73
Hari-Raya Hadji 73
Hari-Raya Puasa 72
health 114–20
hepatitis 119
history 18–44
    pre-Spanish period 19–21
    Spanish colonization 21–7
    American period 28–33
    Republic of the Philippines 33–6
    Marcos years 36–9
    Philippines today 39–45
HIV/AIDS 120
hiya (sense of shame) 52–4
household help 89–92, 114, 119
    emergency loans 93
housing 74–7

Iloilo, Panay Island 71
Islamic festivals 72–3

jeepneys 108–9
jueteng (lottery-style game) 101

Kalibo, Panay Island 71
karaoke 103, 150
kinship ties 27

Laguna 113
Lake Taal 113
language 9, 11, 26, 30, 137, 152–7
    English 154–6
    Filipino 153–4
    in the media 156–7

    Spanish and Chinese 156
Lent 65
literacy 10
loss of face 52, 54–5, 162, 163, 164
lotteries 101
Luzon 10, 12, 14, 17, 18

Mactan Island 21, 113
Makati 75
making the right impression 59
malaria 118
management style 135–40
    expressing and managing disagreement 139–40
mañana 57–8
Manila 9, 10, 12, 13, 15, 16, 17, 40, 47, 75, 82, 94, 96, 97, 101, 108, 109, 111, 112, 113, 115, 117, 122, 123, 125
marriage 48–9, 81
Maynilad 22
meals
    business entertaining 86–7
    in a Filipino home 87–8
media 11, 156–7
medical care 121–5
medicine 123–5
meetings 144–5
Metro Manila 75, 77, 113, 157
Mindanao 10, 12, 17, 21, 29, 37, 41, 45, 63, 104, 112, 113, 125, 126
motivational address 142–3
Mount Mayon 17
Mount Pinatubo 16
music 102
Muslims 11, 63

name, official 10
natural disasters 16–18
negotiations 145–6
New Year 73
nightlife 101–3

office etiquette and protocol 130–35

pabaon tradition 88
Pagsanjan 113

pakikipagkapwa (need for smooth interpersonal relationships) 51–2
pakikisama (desire to be accepted by the group) 51
Palawan 12, 113, 126
Panay Island, Western Visayas 70, 71
pasalubong 151
pool 98
population 10, 45
postal service 158–9
presentations 141, 144
Protestants 11, 61

quality control 137

rail transport 111
Ramadan 72
relationship-based society 50–55, 94
religion 11, 19, 23, 60–63
renting 76
road transport 106–111
robbery 128

safety 125–9
Santo Niño 69, 70, 71, 72
shopping 94–5
singing 7, 150
Sinulog festival 71–2
smiles 163–4
soccer 97–8
socializing 82
speeches 141
spirits 62
sports and games 95–9
stomach upsets 116–17
Subic/Olongapo 113
Sulu 42
swimming pools 119

Taal volcano 113
table manners 105

Tagalog 152–53
Tagaytay 97, 113
Tawi-Tawi 42
taxis 110–111
teamwork 134–5
telephone 11, 157–8
terrain 10
terrorism 125–6
time 11
timekeeping 57–8, 87, 133–4
toilets 115
traffic congestion 77, 106, 108, 109, 115
transport
    air 112
    ferries and boats 111–12
    rail 111
    road 106–111
tribes 19
tricksters 126–7
tuberculosis 119
typhoid fever 115, 120
typhoons 17–18

utang na loob (reciprocation of a favor) 49–50, 147

vaccination 119
Valentine's Day 73
video/TV 11
videoke 103
Visayas 10, 12, 112
volcanoes 16–17

wakes 85–6, 139
water 116, 120
weddings 82–4
women at work 149–50

yaya (nursemaid) 80, 91